GOSWAMI TULSIDAS

GREAT SAINTS OF INDIA SERIES

GOSWAMI TULSIDAS

By

O.P. Ralhan

ANMOL PUBLICATIONS PVT. LTD.
NEW DELHI - 110 002 (INDIA)

ANMOL PUBLICATIONS PVT. LTD.
4374/4B, Ansari Road, Daryaganj
New Delhi - 110 002
Ph.: 23261597, 23278000
Visit us at: www.anmolpublications.com

Goswami Tulsidas

First Published, 2004

ISBN 81-261-1827-X

PRINTED IN INDIA

Published by J.L. Kumar for Anmol Publications Pvt. Ltd., New Delhi - 110 002 and Printed at Mehra Offset Press, Delhi.

Contents

Preface

When Tulsidas was born Northern India was governed by Lodi Dynasty. Bahlol Lodi (1451-1489). His successor was Sikandar Lodi who ruled from 1489-1517. He was succeeded by Ibrahim Lodi (1517-1526). Guru Nanak Dev Ji (1469-1539) had witnessed the foundation of the Mughal Empire in India laid by Babar (1526-1530), who was succeeded by his son, Humayun (1530-1540), during the life time of the Guru.

From the tenth century onwards, successive hordes of Muslim invaders had poured in from Central Asia. As the high way to Delhi through the Punjab the great suffering had been caused to the people of this province. The Afghans and Turks established their rule and various Muslim dynasties ruled Northern India. Foreign rulers and their foreign functionaries ruled through their military strength. They exploited the people are fleeced them. They committed untold atrocities, imposed *Jazia* (a personal tax on all non-Muslims) and otherwise taxed them heavily. All avenues to higher service were closed to the Hindus, who could not get employment except to the lowest posts. Hindu temples were razed to the ground and a large number of Muslim mosques were erected. Hindu schools were closed and every effort was made to crush Hindu culture and civilization. A great many Hindus were converted to Islam on the point of the sword and the spirit of the people was crushed. There was a wide gulf created between the rulers and the ruled and between the Hindus and the Muslim population, so much so that Hindu saints were subjected to all types of humiliations and were made to dress differently from the Muslim saints. There were complete segregation between the Hindus and the Muslims, their rites, customs and ceremonies and their way of living. The masses were greatly demoralised and emasculated. Not a single leader of note was produced by the Hindus during the past five centuries. During this time a very low status was assigned to the Hindus. They were required to put marks on their forehead or attach other distinguishing marks to their dress. They were forbidden to eat grain of a superior quality, to wear rich apparel or to ride good horses, or in palanquins and carriages. In Dera Ghazi Khan district a Hindu could ride only a donkey. The law of blasphemy was strictly enforced and capital punishment was inflicted for any criticism of Islam. Bodhan Brahman was executed by Sikandar Lodi (1485-1517) for saying that Hinduism was as good a religion as Islam. Conversion of Hindus was a frequent occurrence and it was done on a mass scale on occasion and in certain parts of the country.

Guru Nanak was 20 years old when Sikandar Lodi ascended the throne. Even as a Prince, he had been a bigoted Muslim and wanted to kill all the Hindus who had assembled at Thanesar for a bath in the sacred tank. Praising of him Abdulla, the author of *Tarikh-e Daudi,* writes. "He was so zealous a Musalman that he utterly destroyed diverse places of the infidels, and left not a vestige remaining of them. He entirely ruined the shrines of Mathura, the mines of heathenism and turned their principal places of worship into carvan sarais and colleges. Their stone images were given to butchers for using as weights for weighing meat and all the Hindus were strictly prohibited from shaving their heads and beards and performing their ablutions. He thus put an end to all idolatrous rites of the infidels there, and no Hindu, if he wished to have his head or beard shaved, could get a barber to do it. Every city thus conformed as he desired to the custom of Islam". The famous idols of Nagarkot and Jawalamukhi were broken to pieces, which were given to butchers.

Political conditions were much worse. As pointed out by Guru Nanak:- "This age is like a dragon sword—the kings are butchers; Goodness had taken wings and flown". He adds: "There is no one who receiveth or giveth not bribes. The king administers justice only when his palm has been greased (filled)".

Guru Nanak (1469-1539) was also an eye-witness to the treatment meted out to the people by the Mughal invaders in 1521. He was on his way back after touring the Muslim countries. He must have had some idea of the preparations Babar had been making in Afghanistan for invading the Punjab, which he had twice in 1505 and in 1519. On both these occasions Nanak was not in the Punjab. He was returning from his tour on foot not far behind the invaders who came on Irani and Iraqi horses. Before reaching his home town, he stayed at Sayyidpur (now known as Eminabad) with his favourite disciple, Lalo, about 50 miles from Lahore in Gujranwala district.

Babar arrived at Sayyidpur shortly afterwards. Nanak was then still there. The town was mostly inhabited by rich Hindu traders and zamindars. They offered considerable resistance in order to save themselves from surrendering their wealth and women. The infuriated Babar, ordered a general massacre of the people. All the young women were reduced slavery. Others were forced to grind corn and cook food for troops. The town was looted and then destroyed by fire. Guru Nanak and Lalo were forced to carry heavy loads of looted property on their heads to the camp and then compelled to grind corn.

The barbarous treatment of prisoners in the camp, particularly of women, broke the tender heart of Guru Nanak. The shock and pain were too acute for him to bear.

Even before Guru Nanak Devji; Kabir Sahib (1398-1518 A.D.). The symbol of Hindu Muslim unity was prosecuted by Sikandar Lodi (1489-1517 A.D.). The plain speaking of Kabir Sahib and his general disregard for the conventions of society raised up enemies on every side. According to Kabir Panthi tradition it was Shaikhs Taqqi who voiced the feelings of Muhammadans. The famous Pir came before the Emperor Sikandar Lodi and accused Kabir of laying claim to divine attributes. He urged that such conduct merited the penality of death. The Emperor issued a warrant for his arrest and sent men to bring him to the court. Not till evening could the men who were sent persuade Kabir to accompany them. Kabir stood before the Emperor in silence. The Qazi exclaimed, "why do you not salute the Emperor, you Kaffir". Kabir replied, "Those only are Pirs who realise the pain of others, those who cannot are Kaffirs". The Emperor asked him why, when ordered to appear in the morning, he had not come till evening. Kabir replied that he had seen a sight which arrested his attention. The Emperor asked what kind of sight could justify him in disregarding his commands. Kabir rejoined that he had been watching a string of camels passing through a street narrower than the eye of a needle. The Emperor said that he was a liar. Kabir replied, "O Emperor, realise how great is the distance between heaven and earth. Innumerable elephants and camels may be contained in the space between the sun and the moon, and all can be seen through the pupil of the eye which is smaller than the eye of the needle". The Emperor was satisfied and left him go.

The orthodox Brahmins called him irreligious and carried tales of his intimacy with a woman of ill fame. Upon this the Emperor ordered that Kabir should be put to death. He was accordingly put to chains and placed on a boat which was filled with stones. The boat sank but Kabir reappeared as a boy floating down the stream on a leopard's skin. He was again captured and an attempt was made to burn him alive; this attempt, too, did not succeed. He was then accused of witchcraft and the people demanded that he should be trampled to death by an infuriated elephant. Between the elephant and Kabir there appeared a lion at whose sight the elephant fled. There are numerous such legends about Kabir Sahib; some are recorded in the accounts written by his disciples and followers.

Such was the religious and political situation of the country. Just imagine if the living Gods of that period like Kabir Sahib (1398-1518 A.D.) and Shri Guru Nanak Dev Ji Maharaj (1469-1539 A.D.) were treated and tortured in such a barbarious fashion what could have been the fate of the common men?

In these circumstances when the country was passing through a jungle Raj Goswami Tulsidasji was born (1497-1623). Tulsidas himself does not mention the date of his own birth or the name of his birth place. Baba Beni Madho Das mention Samwat 1554 (1497 A.D.) as his date of birth. According to H.H.

Wilsons, he was born in Samwat 1600 (1543 A.D.). Their is, however, a fair consensus among scholars in favour of Bhadrapad 11, 'Mangalwar Samwat 1589 (Tuesday, September 18, 1532 A.D. It is a date which Sir George Grierson and a host of the best modern scholars consider most likely. Shiv Singh Sengar in his Shiva Singh Saroj states that Tulsidas was born "near about Samwat 1583" which is a date not far from Samwat 1589 (1532 A.D.). But 1497 A.D. has been approved the authenticated date by majority of the scholars. During this period Northern India was being governed by Sikandar Lodi (1489-1517). It means when Shri Guru Nanak Dev Ji went to his heavenly abode (Jyoti Jot Samaye) on September 22, 1539 A.D., Tulsidasji was of about 42 years old, and at that time after Sikandar Lodi (1489-1517 A.D.) than Ibrahim Lodi (1517-1526) and then Mughal Emperor Babar (1526-1530) and Emperor Humayun (1530-1540) was the ruler. And similarly when Kabir Sahib breathed his last in the year 1518 Ibrahim Lodi (1517-1526) was the ruler of India and Tulsidasji was of about 21 years old.

During Guru Angad's time (1539 A.D. to 1552 A.D.) Humayun (1530-1540 A.D.) came to the throne of India. He had to fight two consecutive battles against Sher Shah Suri (1542-1545) and was defeated in the second battle. Near Kanauj, he suffered yet another defeat and was obliged to flee from India. He made his way to Lahore. At Lahore he enquired for some priest who could perform miracles and help him regain his throne. He was informed of the greatness of the late Guru Nanak and his successor Guru Angad and advised to seek the latter's assistance.

Humayun then proceeded to Khadur to meet the Guru. At that time the Guru was in deep meditation while his minsterls were playing and singing the Guru's hymns. The Emperor was kept standing. He was offended and, in a fit of rages, put his hand on the hilt of the sword and drew it out of the scabbard. He wanted to cut of the Guru's head with the sword. The Guru opened his eyes and looked at Humayun. Then he smiled and said "When you should have used your sword against Sher Shah, you failed to do so. Now when you come amongst the man of God, instead of saluting them respectfully, you desire to draw your sword on them. You fled from the battlefield in a cowardly manner and now you are posing as a hero who wishes to attack religious men".

Humayun hung his head in shame and craved the Guru's spiritual assistance. The Guru said, "I shall pray for you. You will get back your kingdom after sometime. But do not forget God even then. Be a just and kind ruler. After Sher Shah Suri (1542-1545 A.D.) Islam Shah ruled during (1545-1553).

Hence Tulsidasji (1497-1623) happens to see the period of Guru Nanak (1469-1539), the Guruship of Guru Angad (1539-March 29, 1552). Guru Angad was born on March 31, 1504. Guru Amar Das (1552 A.D. September 1, 1574). Guru Amar Das was born on May 5, 1479. Guru Ram Das (1574-1581) Guru Ram Das was born in the year 1534 A.D.). Guru Arjun Dev (September 1, 1581 A.D. to May 30, 1606). Guru Arjun Dev was born on April 15, 1563 and Guru Hargobind (May 25, 1606–March 3, 1644). Guru Hargobind was born on June 14, 1595 A.D. and contemporary ruler:-

1. Sikandar Lodi (1489-1517 A.D.) (Guru Nanak Dev 1469-1539)
2. Ibrahim Lodi (1517-1526 A.D.) (Guru Angad 1539-1552).
3. Emperor Babar (1526-1530 A.D.) (Guru Amar Das 1552-1574).
4. Emperor Humayun (1530-1540 A.D.) (Guru Ram Das 1574-1581).
5. Sher Shah Suri (1542-1545 A.D.) (Guru Arjun Dev 1581-1606)
6. Islam Shah (1545-1553 A.D.) (Guru Hargobind 1606-1644).
7. Emperor Humayun (1554-1556 A.D.)
8. Emperor Akbar (1556-1605 A.D.)
9. Emperor Jahangir (1605-1626 A.D.)

After the death of Akbar on October 17, 1605 his son Jahangir succeeded him. Jahangir was a fanatic Muslim. He was totally intolerant towards other religions. Even the Qazis and Mullahs provoked him against Guru Arjun Dev, and urged him to put an end to Guru Arjun's life.

About the same time, Jahangir's son, Khusro (future Shah Jahan) rebelled against him. He fought against his father but lost the battle and fled to Lahore. Jahangir followed him. He declared that whosoever helped the rebel prince, would be punished.

On his way to Lahore, Jahangir passed through Goindwal and Taran Taran. He tried to enquire from the people if there was anybody who had helped Khusro. The Guru's enemies found a golden chance of their lives and promptly made up a story against the Guru. They said to Jahangir, "Khusro met Guru Arjun at Goindwal and asked for his help. The Guru prayed for his success against Your Majesty and also gave him a large sum of money".

Jahangir was livid with rage. Already the Guru's growing popularity among the Muslims and Hindus alike had aroused suspicion in the mind of Jahangir; and now more than ever, he remembered the promise he had made to the Qazi's to put an end to the Guru's life and activities.

In his autobiography *"The Tuzik-e-Jahangiri"* Jahangir had mentioned:-

A Hindu Arjan by name, lived .... in the garb of a 'Pir' and sheikh and had captivated the hearts of many simple minded Hindus and foolish and stupid Muslims by his ways and means... For three or four generations they had kept this shop warm. For years I have been thinking of either putting an end to this false traffic or that he (Guru Arjun) should be brought into the fold of Islam.

In his autobiography, Jahangir also referred to the allegations against the Guru for having blessed his rebellious son Khusro.

The Emperor Jahangir ordered the Guru to be brought before him and put to death. Chandu an enemy of Guru Arjun said, 'I shall carry out the Emperor's orders. I have made up my plans. Give the Guru into my hands and I shall kill him with tortures.

For five days the Guru was tortured in various ways. The Emperor's officers poured burning sand on him, seated him in a red-hot cauldron and bathed him with boiling water. The Guru bore all these tortures without a sigh or groan. During the torture period Guru kept repeating the following prayer:

> "When very great troubles befall, and no body recievth one;
>
> When enemies pursue, and relations flee away; when all from whom man looked for assistance have fled, and all succours are at an end; If he then remembers God, no hot wind shall strike him".

Several jogis and religious men appealed for the release of the Guru. Mian Mir, the Muslim saint, whom even Jahangir respected went to see his friend Guru Arjun and said to him, "May I appeal to the Emperor for your release ? May I ask him to punish these people who are torturing you"?

The Guru replied, "No brother. All is happening according to God's will. Men who stand for truth have to suffer often. Their suffering gives strength to the cause of truth. Go, brother, pray for me. Pray for the success of my cause. Pray for victory to Truth.

On the 5th day, the Guru was taken to the river Ravi. With its ice cold water he bathed his feet and hands. Then he went into the river and bathed his whole body. All along, he was reciting the Japji Sahib. Before leaving his mortal coil, he declared his son Shri Hargobind as his successor.

The death of Guru Arjun angered the Sikhs as much that they changed from a peaceful religious sect into a community of warriors who were ready to defend their religious faith with the sword if needed.

Jahangir grew jealous of his power and popularity of Guru Hargobind (1595-1644). He expressed his fears to his ministers, who had already been briefed by Chandu to speak against the Guru. Due to the conspiracy of Chandu Guru Hargobind was imprisoned in the Gwalior prison.

It is however, difficult to substantiate or disbelieve entirely the strory about Tulsidasji's visit to the Mughal Emperor in Delhi. It is said that Emperor Jahangir on hearing about the miracles he had performed asked the poet to be his guest and to demonstrate his powers. The official historians of the day make no mention of his and the vague hints thrown out by the poet are not enough to give us a clear picture of what really took place. Priyadas in his commentry on the Bhaktmal says that when the poet met "the Badshah of Delhi" and the latter asked him to show miracles, Tulsidas replied "These stories about miracles are false. One should put one's faith in Rama alone". which certainly is a reply in the poet's characteristic manner.

Tulsidas's reputation as a devotee who had seen "Bhagwan Shri Ram" face to face at Chitrakut seems to have travelled and reached the people of Kashi before him. Naturally when the Ram Charit Manas was completed and came to the notice of the people, it received instant and wide recognition on account of the author's love of 'Shri Ram', his absorption in the theme, the freshness of his approach, his deep humanity and the music and the movement of his flowing verses. It also aroused controversy because a work of the deepest import and obvious merit was written not in Sanskrit, the sacred language, but in the language of the people, because it attempted a synthesis of conflicting schools of thought and belief and, above all, because of its emphasis on a simple and direct faith, free from complicated ritual and set of observances. That is why Goswami Tulsidasji is worshiped in every household of India.

I am lucky enough that my publisher Shri Kumar Sahib have assigned this prestigious job to undertake the biography of such a Saint of high reputation who had direct links with Pawanputtra 'Hanuman', Bhagwan Shri Ram and had been blessed by Lord Shiva and helped and nursed by Maa Parvati.

I am grateful of all those authors and Publishers from which I have took notes and references from their books on Goswami Tulsidasji. I am indebted to Shri S.P. Bahadur and Ms. Chander Kumari Handoo from who's works I took the liberty to have copied few stanza's translated from Hindi to English.

I am also grateful of my old colleagues at Nehru Memorial Library, Teen Murti House, New Delhi Shri Naveen Mahajan,

Shri Bhagwan Das, Shrimati Shashi Anand, Smt. Asha Arora and Smt. Seema Mathur without their kind cooperation, help and guidance this book would not have been completed.

Being a Ram Bhakat from my very childhood, I have tried my level best to collect and produce best material on Goswami Tulsidasji. All the merits are of this God sent Saint in this Kaliyug and all the shortcoming and faults are of mine. I hope the readers of this book will forgive me for the errors and shortcomings and go through this sacred book with great and deep devotion.

New Delhi O.P. Ralhan

1

Goswami Tulsidas

(The Celebrated Author of *Ram Charitmanas*)

Childhood and Education

In *Ram Charit Manas* Goswami Tulsidasji's brief life sketch is recorded as under. There is a village named Rajapur in the district of Banda near Prayag. In this village one Atma Ram Dube named person who belonged to a well known Saryupareen Brahman caste lived. The name of his wife was Hulsi. In Samwat 1554 on the eve of Shravan Shukla Saptami, Abhuktmool Nakshattar, this most fortunate couple was blessed with a son who was born after 12 months pregnancy. At the time of his birth he did not wept, but on the contrary he uttered word 'Ram' from his mouth. There were thirty two teeths in his mouth. His physic looked like a five years old child. By seeing such a strange child his father's heart filled with evil and started guessing various things. His mother named Hulsi was equally upset. She feared the worst, and on the 10th day's of her son's birth she handed over to him to his devoted maid servant, Muniya to whisk away the child at the dead of night to maid's-in-laws across the river and thus save him from death. The maid obliged. The next day Hulsi, the mother breathed her last. The maid servant's mother-in-law who's name was Chuniya looked after the child properly. When Tulsidas was about 5½ years old, Chuniya also died. The child became orphan. The child roamed about aimlessly in the streets. Seeing him in such a desperate condition Mata Parvati have mercy on such a brilliant chap named Tulsidas. She used to come to him daily in the guise of a Brahmani and feed him with her own hands.

On the other hand by the blessing of Lord Shiva, Shri Narhariyanandji who was a devoted devotee of Shri Anantanandji, and was living at Ramshailpur searched this child and named him as "Rambola". He took him to Ayodhya and there in Samwat 1561 Magh Shukal Panchami on a Friday his Yagopaveet (sacred thread) ceremony was performed. Without any coaching the child Rambola recited "Gayatri Mantar" of his own. Seeing this all the assembled persons were surprised. After the ceremony Swami Narhari performed five customs of Vaishaves, he gave diksha (Name of God) of Rammantar to Rambola and kept him at Ayodhya for further studies. The child Rambola was very sharp in studies. Whatsoever was taught by his teacher he used to learn by heart. After staying at Ayodhya for a certain period both the Guru and the disciple reached Sukar Kshetra (Soron). At this place Shri Narhariji recited Ramcharit to Tulsidas. After few days they left for Kashi. At Kashi he stayed with Sheshsanatanji for 15 years and studied Vedas and Vedantas. Now he was a grown up chap. With the due permission of his Guru he left for his birth place. On reaching there he noticed that every thing of his family has ruined. He performed last rites of his parents with full devotion and according to Hindu rites. While staying at his home town he used to recite Ramkatha to the residents[1].

According to Mahipati, Now listen, O hearers. While Narayan was reclining on the serpent Shesh in the sea of milk, some of his bhaktas arrived. Udhav, Akrur, Valmiki, Dhruva, Prahlada and Shuka coming near Him paid their reverence to the Lord of the Yadavas. The Saviour of the world said to Valmiki, 'In the Kaliyug sins have become intolerable. I wish you to become an avtar among mortals and bring about the salvation of men. The Ramayana which you composed, in which you sang my name, goodness, and good deeds, was in the Sanskrit language which the ignorant people of the Kaliyug did not understand. So becoming an avatar among mortals, set them to worshipping me. Valmiki hearing Him say this made obeissance to Him. In the northern part of the country, in the city of Hastanapur (Delhi) in the house of a Kanoja Brahman the Rishi Valmiki became a voluntary avatar. The Brahman bore the name of Atmaram. He became a man devoted to religion and of perfect good deeds. Akbar was king at that time, and he was in the service of Akbar. Atmaram was a wise Brahman and he enjoyed the King's favour. It was in his family that Valmiki became an avatar. The good Brahman Atmaram, performed rituals of birth and naming of his son. He was named Tulsi. The father lovingly played with him. Day by day he grew in stature. His parents invested him with the sacred thread. And he was kept as a Brahmachari (a celibate) for twelve years. They made him study the Vedas according to the prescribed rules.[2]

Baba Beni Madhavadasa has recorded in his book entitled Mula Gosain Carita by saying that the ancient saint Valmiki cursed by Hanuman, was reborn as Tulsi for the good of the world. How he incurred the displeasure of Hanuman, though not of primary importance to our narrative may be retold here. Like a tiny seed from which grows the mighty banyan tree is the name of God or Rama. The whole creation evolves out of it and is withdrawn into it again. Fearing perhaps that this philosophical and spiritual truth would not be understood by the ordinary man, Valmiki requested Hanuman not to reveal it to all and sundry. Baba Beni Madhavdasa does not say why Hanuman was displeased, but we imagine that it may be because he sensed an undercurrent of spiritual arrogance in the request. But the curse or anger of the great ones is really a blessing in disguise, and this also was not without a purpose of its own. Valmiki was born in this age of Kali to repeat once more the life history of Shri Rama Babaji, his obviously ardent disciple, read the Mula Gosain Carita as a matter of routine, for in his opinion a study of the life of his teacher was sure to fill the heart with the love of God. In his devotion he is moved to say, "He who reads the Mula Gosain Carita every day will through the grace of Siva, Parvati and Hanuman, attain devotion to Rama. In the next and last verse of the book he further adds, 'In Samwat 1687 (A.D. 1630' and seven years after the death of Tulsi) on the ninth day of the month of Kartika, Beni Madhavadas composed this for his daily recitation.[3]

Tulsi's date and time of birth is stated by Baba Beni Madhavadasa is as follows:- 'When the Sun was in its own house (Leo), Jupiter was in Cancer, with the Moon in (one of the four) moveable Zodiac signs (Cara rasi), the planet Mars was in the seventh house, Saturn in the eighth house, during the time of Abhihit (naksatra or muhurta) and in the pleasant hours of the evening Tulsidasa was born on the banks of the Jamuna. It was the month of August (Sravana) in Samwat 1554 (A.D. 1497)[4].

In his book entitled 'Kavitavali', which he wrote in his later years, Tulsidas writes:-

> His father and mother brought him into the world and abandoned him.
>
> Destiny has written nothing good upon his forehead, He was low, a vessel for disrespect a coward who was glad to get, even the scraps thrown out for dogs[5].

The interpretation generally given of this passage is that the poet was born on an inauspicious day and as a result his parents felt obliged to disown their new born baby as an impure and untouchable child. Such an interpretation is corborated by another statement found in Vinaya-Patrika:

> And as the wretched snake casts off its
> slough, so did my father and mother
> abandon me....
> They forced even to touch my shadow
> such was my fortune[6].
> In Kavitavali Tulsidas has said:
> I was born in a family of beggars,
> when the band played in celebration,
> My father and mother hearing felt
> anguish and remorse[7]

About his childhood, Tulsidas makes only one reference indicating that he was rescued by saints i.e. believers of Rama:

> I told my poverty at every door,
> I gnashed my teeth and fell at feet;
> till some holy men (Saints) saw my
> misery and said:

Sorrow no mores, Rama is the refuge, of wretches[8].

According to the Gautamacandrika, whose author, Krsna Dutta was a contemporary of Tulsidas, Narharidas lived on the banks of the river Narmada and at Sukarakheta. This has been confirmed by the information given in the Ramacharitmanas that, as a child, Tulsidas heard from his guru at Sukara Khera, the story of Rama, which because of his tender age he was at first unable to understand[9].

Nabhadas the author of The Bhakta Mala writes concerning Tulsidas:-

> For the salvation of being in this perverse Dark Age Valmiki has become Tulsi;
>
> In the former Treta age he made the thousand million verses of the Ramayana.
>
> of which but one letter can redeem even a man who has slain a Brahman.
>
> Now he has again published abroad God's many wonders as a comfort for all devotees,
>
> And intoxicated with the love of Rama's feet he repeats his Name both night and day according to his vow. Thus he has secured an easily accessible boat for crossing the boundaries ocean of existence.
>
> For the salvation of beings in this perverse Dark Age Valmiki has become Tulsi[10].

According to a popular tradition, Tulsidas was born at Rajapur in the Banda district. However, others have suggested either Hajipur in near Chitrakuta, Tari in Doab, Sukarakheta or Ayodhya in the Faizabad district or Soron in the Etah district[11]. Tulsidas himself does not mention the date of his own birth or the name of his birth place and there is no entirely reliable or indisputably authentic evidence to enable us to fix firm dates and place names. Scholars relying mainly on the testimony of Baba Beni Madho Das mention Samwat 1554 (1497 A.D.) as his date of birth, while H.H. Wilson's remark in one of his papers that Tulsidas "Commenced his Hindi version of the Ramayan in the year of Samwat 1631 when he was thirty one years of age" has persuaded many that he was born in Samwat 1600 (1543 A.D.). Various references are given in support of both the dates but the reliability of both is open to question in view of what the poet himself has said about the circumstances of his life.

There is, however, a fair consensus among scholars in favour of Bhadrapad 11, Mangalwar Samwat 1589 (Tuesday, September 18, 1532 A.D.). It is a date which Sir George Grierson and a host of the best modern scholars consider most likely. Shiv Singh Sengar in his Shiv Singh Saroj states that Tulsidas was born "near about Samwat 1585" which is a date not far removed from Samwat 1589 (1532 A.D.). The date also happens to stand the test of astrological calculations perfectly.

The controversy over the exact birth place of Tulsidas is not so easily set at rest. Seven cities claimed the honour of the birth place of Homer and nearly as many are mentioned as the birth place of Tulsidas.

All these places belong to Uttar Pradesh and out of the four most after mentioned three are situated within a fairly restricted area near Chitrakut. Sir George Grierson, who had good sources of information and the ability to subject them to dispassionate examination, was of the view that Tari on the banks of the Yamuna and only ten or twelve miles away from Rajapur had the best claim. One of the commentaries on the Bhaktmal has it that he was born in Tari and that subsequently he took up residence in Rajapur. It is account widely prevalent in circles devoted to the study and recitation of the Ramayana.

There is next the more generally accepted claim of Rajapur to be recognised as the birth place of Tulsidas. The Imperial Gazetteer of India states simply "According to tradition the town was founded by Tulsidas, the celebrated author of the Ramayana". The statement lends colour to the assertion of the commentator on the Bhakatmal that the poet was born actually a few miles away at Tari but that subsequently after he had seen some of the vicissitudes of life, he went over to Rajapur to set himself up there and sing the praises of Ram. In any case, there are many facts and circumstances pointing to the poets' association with Rajapur in his younger years which it is not easy to ignore. The presence of a house in which Tulsidas is said to have lived, an image of God Hanuman he is said to have set up, a copy of Ayodhya Kand of the Ram Charit Manas, some families which trace their descent from a disciple of the poet and documents relating to land grants provide good support to the claim of Rajapur. The fact is not to be missed that most of the older biographers of the poet including Baba Beni Madho Das, a life long companion and disciple of the poet, have stated that Rajapur was his birth place and some of the most authoritative modern scholars agree with the statement of Shiva Singh Sengar in his book that Tulsidas was a resident of Rajapur".

There is also an interesting episode in the Ayodhya Kand of the Ram Charit Manas. Just at the moment Shri Ram crosses the Yamuna and enters the territory near about Rajapur an unnamed young ascetic appears on the scene. The intensity of this ascetics devotional fervour as he falls at the feet of Shri Ram has led some commentators to identify him with the poet himself who would naturally be moved powerfully by the sight of his Lord and Master landing on ground associated with his own birth place. It is difficult to explain why the poet should have held up the narrative to introduce, rather dramatically a character who was nothing to do with the rest of the story, unless he had some deeply sentimental and personal reasons for doing so[12].

It will not be out of place to mention here that when Hulasi, the mother of Tulsi on the fourth day of his birth took a turn for the worst. She was already aware of the superstitious talk that had been going on amongst the menfolk. In case she died, she feared that the little one would be looked upon as bringing bad luck to the family. As stated earlier she then called her maid servant, Muniya gave her all her ornaments and jewellery and begged her to take the child away to her village in Haripur and look after him as her own son. Muniya agreed and left quietly at the dead of night with the precious little bundle in her arms. Hulasi was heart broken at the seperation from her son. Her condition deteriorated rapidly and she felt that her end was approaching. After praying Brahma, Vishnu and Mahesh to look after her infant son, she breathed her last early the next morning on the eleventh (ekadasi) day.

It would be a great injustice to Muniya, the maid servant of Hulasi, if it is not brought to light that how she performed her journey from Rajapur to Haripur. She travelled the whole night and arrived safely at her village home two hours after dawn.

Relating the pathetic story of the child to her mother-in-law, Chuniya, she requested the father to look after the little one. The elder woman's motherly heart was touched and she said, 'You have done well; there is a cow in the house and the motherless child will thriqe on the milk'. She looked after him lovingly and always tried to keep him happy. As ill luck would have it, after five years and five months, when Ram Bola had learnt to walk and talk, the foster mother died suddenly of snakebite. Message was sent to his father, Atmarama, informing him of Chuniya's death and offering to send Rama Bola to him, but the hard hearted father was unmoved by his son's sad plight and refused to take him back. He said he could not give shelter to such an unfortunate child, two of whose guardians had died so early and who seemed to be fated to lose those who loved and protected him. So he wandered about like a destitute begging for food and receiving only harsh and unkind treatment from the world. He was recorded the darkest days of his life in the following stanzas in Kavitavali and Vinay Patrika[13].

Nurtured in sin, and suffering humiliation
through extreme poverty
My possessions were a duty and patched quilt and
an earthen water pot[14].
Mother and father, giving birth to me in the world,
cast me off.
Even Brahma did not give me a good destiny,
Lowly and cowardly, spurned by all,
I longed for the piece of bread in mouth of a dog[15].
Mother and father abandoned me at birth,
And bereft of good Karma
The Creater made my path a tormented one,

Without the Name (of God) I wandered,
Greedy to fill my stomach.
Even sorrow suffered to see my misery.
Like a dog I licked many a leaf plate.
But my stomach was never filled.
From door to door I went begging
Baring my teeth (in a painful attempt to smile)
Falling at the feet (of those from whom I begged).
There are kind people who are powerful,
And can destroy the shortcomings and misery
of the world in its ten directions,
But none of them spoke to me.
My parents abandoned me, as the snake,
That gives up its offspring at birth,
Why should I be angry ?
Whom should I blame ?
It is all my own misfortune.
People feared to contact my shadow.
Though I was your personal servant,
Yet, led by hope, I offered
My services to those of impure hearts.
Bewailing my lot,
Dwelling on my poverty,
I wandered from door to door,
But not even ashes were thrown into my open mouth
Without food and clothing
I ran here and there as if demented.
Giving up self-respect, dearer than life,
I showed my empty stomach at all moments,
To the wicked ones.
O Lord ! dragged on by avarice.
I received nothing.
Truly I tell you for the smallest gain
Unashamed I danced to every tune.
(Lured on by lowly greed)[16].
I went from house to house
Like a beggar for a piece (of bread)
O thou kind one (Hanuman), guardian of the poor.
Thou protectedst me as a child[17].

Baba Bani Madhavdasa says that by reason the grace of Parvati to Rama Bola, Siva felt obliged to arrange for the boy's future. He appeared to Narharidasa in a vision and related to him the life history of Shri Rama. He then revealed Rama Bola's whereabouts to this hollyman and said that from now onwards the education and protection of the boy would be a charge on Naraharidasa. Further, Siva said that the sadhu was to take Rama Bola to Ayodhya, initiate him in the mystics formula of Rama's name (Rama Mantra) and repeat to him the life history of Rama. Delighted to be chosen as the instrument of the divine will, Naraharidasa went to Haripur, located the boy and with the consent of the villagers took him over. Rama Bola sat on his lap and lovingly the sadhu said to him, 'Do not be anxious any more. God will look after you in every way'. Soon both of them left for Ayodhya, and in Samwat 1561 (A.D. 1505), in the month of Phalguna (February), on holy Vasanta Panchami day (Friday), the sacred thread ceremony of Rama Bola was performed on the banks of the Sarayu river. To the astonishment of all those present on the occasion, this gifted child recited the Gayatri mantar without being taught. After this he was ceremonially given the Rama Mantra by Narharidasa, who then started his education in right earnest. The teacher was pleased to find that Rama Bola's intelligence and memory were for above the average. Seeing his devotional temperament and desire to serve, the teacher (guru) blessed his little pupil from the bottom of his heart. When Rama Bola related the sufferings of his life, the sadhus eyes filled with tears. He clasped the boy to his heart and comforted him as best as he could.

After a stay of ten months in Ayodhya, master and disciple left for Sukar Khet—a place of pilgrimage at the confluence of the Sarayu and Ghagra rivers. Here both of them lived in close association and it was in this place that Rama Bola first heard the fascinating story of his chosen deity (Ishetdeva), Rama, whose divinely human life he was destined to narrate and interpret to the world later on. The following lines of the Ramacharitmanasa support this account.

I heard this story from my Guru in Sukar Khet, but being a mere child and unconscious (of God), I was unable to grasp it[18].

Tulsi further says:

Teacher and taught should be,
The treasure house of wisdom
For the story of Rama is deep,
How can I understand it ?
Who am I but an ignorant creature
Dulled by the impurities of Kali ?
Stil my teacher repeated it,
Over and over again,
And I understood a little
In keeping with my intelligence[19].

The guru and the chela (disciple) stayed in Sukar Khet for five years, after which they started on their journey once again. One day they reached the holy city of Benaras and halted at Ganga Ghat where once Shri Ramanand had spent some time. At this ghat one another sadhu named Shesh Sanatan, the most respected South Indian Sanskrit scholar in Kashi of his time, even at first sight he was very much attracted to the bright and winning ways of Rama Bola, and he requested Narharidasa to allow him to take over the guardianship of the boy. A little unwilling, Narharidas was persuaded. And it was saint Shesh Sanatan who taught Tulsidas the four Vedas, the Puranas, the Sastras, the Six Philosophies, history, poetry and other branches of learning. According to Gautam Chandrika the guru's name was Anand Kanan. Kashi during that period attracted scholars and saints from all over India. They used to come to participate in philosophical discourses and debates.

On the request of Shesh Sanatana, Narharidas called Rama Bola, handed him over to Shesh Sanatana and went back to Chitrakut himself which place he had originally left for the sake of this orphan boy. Rama Bola remained with his Guru for six years. During this period he acquired good knowledge in Pananis Sanskrit grammar. His studies came to an end with the death of the veteran saint. Due to the irony of fate he was left alone in the world, but this time due to his deep devotion to his studies, kind and loving affection of his guru he was now a well read man with a mature mind. Thus due to the blessings and loveable care of Rama Bola by Swami Narharidasa who sowed the seeds of moral values and devotion to God Almighty in his tender heart and Swami Shesh Sanatana made him a complete man in every respect to face this world.

I have quoted some of the relevant incidents, even at the risk of repetition to enable the learned scholars and readers of this book, to acquiant them with sufferings and hardships of this celebrated author, brilliant poet and saintly son of India, quoted and recorded by various renowned authors in their own style and manner[20].

Notes and References

Birth and Childhood

1. Tulsidas—Ramcharitmanas.
2. Stories of Indian Saints—Translation of Mahipatis Marathi Bhaktavijaya by Dr. Justice E. Abbot and Pandit Narha R. Godbole.
3. Tulsidas—Poet, Saint and Philosopher of the sixteenth century by Chandra Kumari Handoo. Orient Longman, Bombay, p. 8-9.
4. Tulsidasa aur unka yug, p. 306.
5. Kavitavali VII.57 (The passage quoted from the Kavitavali are taken from F.R. Allchins' translation. Allchin F.R. Kavitavali quoted in Tulsidas by C.K. Handoo, p. 8).
6. Vinay Patrika 275—Ibid.
7. Kavitavali—quoted by Chandra Kumari Handoo —Tulsidas, p. 8.
8. Vinay Patrika—Ibid.
9. Tulsidas— Chandra Kumari Handoo—p. 9.
10. Quoted by F.R. Allchin, Kavitavali, p. 40 and quoted by Handoo—Tulsidas, p. 13.
11. Tulsidasa—Chandra Kumari Handoo, p. 14.
12. Tulsidas—Devendra Singh—National Book Trust, New Delhi, p. 4-5. 1971.
13. Tulsidas—Chandra Kumari Handoo.
14. Kavitavali quoted by Ms. Handoo, p. 13.

15. *Ibid.*

16. *Vinay Patrika* quoted by Ms. Handoo in her book Tulsidasa, p. 13.

17. Hanuman Bahuka quoted by Ms. Handoo in her book Tulsidas, p. 14.

18. Mansa quoted by Chandra Kumari Handoo, p. 17-18.

19. *Ibid.*

20. Tulsidas - Chandra Kumari, Handoo and Madan Gopal's article in the book entitled, Ramayana, Mahabharata and Bhagvata writers—General Editor V. Raghvan, Publication Division, 1978.

2

Marriage and Renunciation

The mention of the marriage of Goswami Tulsidas had been made in Ramcharitmanas in these words : During Samwat 1583 Jyeshath on 13 Guruwar he was married with a girl of Bhardwaj gotra and he started living with his newly wedded bride. Once his wife went to his parental house alongwith his brother. Tulsidas also followed her. Seeing this she rebuked him and said, "if you bore half the love that you have for my fleshy body towards Rama, you would surely be freed from the fears and sufferings of human life". These words sank deep in the heart of Tulsidas. He did not stop for a moment there and left the place in no time, and took an irrevocable decision to renounce home and hearth. After leaving his in-laws house Tulsidas reached Prayag. There he get rid of his family life and became a sadhu. After touring various places he reached Kashi. Near Mansrover he witnessed Kakbhushundi. At Kashi Tulsidas started reciting Ramkatha. There he happened to meet a demon, who told him the whereabouts of Hanumanji. After meeting Hanumanji Tulsidas requested to have a glimpse of Raghunathji. Hanumanji told him that you can have 'darshan' of Raghunathji at Chitrakoot. After knowing this Tulsidas left for Chitrakoot[1].

Chandra Kumari Handoo has narrated the story of the marriage of Tulsidas as under: Tulsidasa has completed his studies and he was twenty eight years old. He was eager to visit his home town. One day he reached Rajapur and found his house in ruins. His father had died long ago and no family member was there to welcome him. From his village bhata (bard) he came to know the history of his family and told him how a sadhu had cursed his father, Atmaram, for having forsaken Rama Bola in infancy. The father had died within six months and the other members of the family within ten years of the curse. Villagers were happy to see him in their midst. Tulsidasji built up a hut for himself and started living there, and recited the Ramakatha in the traditional way of the scholarly and devout brahmin priest[2].

Dinabandhu Pathak of Bharadwaja gotra brahmin lived in a village named Tarpita, acorss the river Jamuna, who had a marriageable daughter. Once Dinabandhu, while visiting Rajapur with his family, heard Tulsidas recitation of tho Ramayan. He was so impressed with the devotion, intelligence and handsome bearing of the promising young man that he returned after a few months with a proposal of marriage. Tulsidas was reluctant at first, but the pious and simple old man said with some emphasis and much faith that this was an order he had received from Mother Parvati in a dream. How could he then look for a son-in-law elsewhere? He remained with Tulsidas, fasting completely in protest against his refusal and thus obtained the latter's consent. The wedding was celebrated in Samwat 1583. (A.D. 1526) on the thirteenth day of the bright fortnight in the month of Jeth (May-June) at midnight, when Tulsidas was 28 years and 10 months of age.

Ratnavali was a beautiful bride and Tulsidas loved her a lot. He proved a beautiful husband and could not tolerate separation from her even for a moment. The couple was blessed with a son named Taraka, but unfortunately he died in infancy. This unfortunate event upset their married life.

One day when Tulsidas had gone to a nearby village called Barkhana, Ratnavali's brother came to visit her and she left with him for her parental home without the permission of her husband. On his return he came to know about the departure of his Ratnavali to her parental home, he could not tolerate this separation and decided to follow her. He crossed the river at night, called loudly and knocked hard at the door of his father-in-laws house. The entire household was asleep, but Ratnavali recognising her husbands voice, awoke and opened the door for him[3]. On seeing him the Ratnavali said :-

> If half of your devotion to this skelton,
> Of skin and bones was given to Rama,
> You would surely overcome the fear of the word.[4]

These words of Ratnavali pierced Tulsi's heart like an arrow. He at once retraced his steps from his father-in-laws house. Ratnavali's brother followed him for a long distance, but he could not be turned back. In this moment of disappointment, he suddenly remembered the advice of his Guru:

> If you have your spiritual welfare at heart
> And wish to realise God,
> Keep away from gold and woman,
> Says Narhari[5].

Baba Madhav Das says, that broken hearted, Ratnavali died in Samwat 1589 (A.D. 1532 in the month of Asadha (June-July) on the 11th day of the dark night, Wednesday, exactly after six years of her marriage, and probably a year after Tulsi had left her. Her death caused a great stir in the village community and became a common topic of comment. Among the wise gentry some of them said she was a Saraswati, or the goddess of wisdom, while other commented that God had spoken through her to destroy the delusion of His devotee. In either case her memory was honoured as a woman of deep spirituality, who gave up her personal happiness so that her husband could, without any misgiving, walk firmly and steadily on Godward path. Tradition, however, fondly keeps Ratnavali alive to a ripe old age when once again she meets Tulsi, who is supposed to come unknowingly to her father's house for food and rest. A verse in the Dohavali is ascribed to her. Seeing Tulsidas carrying in a bag gopi-chandana and camphor for his daily worship, she says to him that if he can carry these accessories, he should either carry her alongwith him in his bag or depend on discrimination and renunciation alone[6].

On hearing these words it is said that Tulsi immediately

got rid of the few articles he possessed. But these stories are not seemed authentic.

Mahipati has related this incident in his own style. He said that after searching out a bride for him his marriage took place. As his childhood passed away and he became a young man, the two were united in love. They never could endure separation. Both gave themselves upto enjoying many kinds of rich clothes and ornaments, garlands of pearls and brilliant jewels, saffron, musk, sandal and flowers, yellow betelnut leaves. Cardamons, cloves and nutmeg; but Tulsidas could not endure being without his wife. The name of Tulsidas wife was Devi Mamata. As a dutiful wife she served him with full reverence.

It happened one day, that King Akbar was going on a tour. Tulsidas immediately joined him and went with him. Just then a messenger arrived from her mothers home asking her to come there. He said, 'your mother is seriously ill. Let her have a sight of you and then you can return. On hearing this she wept aloud. Hearing that her mother was seriously ill, she became hysterical. The messenger therefore said to her, we have told you what is false. It is many days since you have visited your mother. Tulsidas refuses to send you, therefore we told you a falsehood'. Mamata replied to them, 'My husband has gone on the royal tour. In the meantime I shall go to my mothers. Having visited her I will immediately return. Obtaining leave from mother and father-in-law Mamta went to visit her own mother. That very day, by evening Tulsidas returned. He questioned his mother and learned all the news. Said, he 'My dear one, why have you left me and gone away? At night on his bed he was unable to sleep. So he started at once and by walking ten miles that night he arrived at the house of his father-in-law. Two (Ghadis) of the night had already passed away. All the doors were closed. Tulsidas looked all about him. Just then he saw a great poisonous serpent hanging down from above. He seized it with his hand and ascended to the upper story. As he entered the house the servants were awakened, and as they looked about they saw Tulsidas. Mamta, that mine of beauty awoke just at that moment. Seeing her husband there, she arose astonished. The husband said, 'You mine of beauty, why did you leave me and come here? I have had to walk ten miles, in order to come for you. The wife replied, 'The Yamuna river is full of flood. I cannot understand how you were able to enter the house. Tulsidas replied, 'Your love for me is so great that you have threw a rope from above and I crossed holding on to it. The dutiful wife hearing this replied, 'why do you speak an untruth? I never threw a rope from the upper storey. As she did not know what was right or wrong, she said, O.K. show me the rope. Taking her servant with her and lighting a lamp they looked for it... They saw a great enormous serpent hanging down from above. All were frightened. She told Tulsidas, you are always intoxicated with your ignorance. She rebuked him for coming at such a time of night. If this serpent had bitten you, you would have lost your life. With a desire to see me you came rushing by night. Many have lost their lives in running after women. Through these words of Mamata, Tulsidas experienced a change of heart, and left her immediately. He remembered all he had done in his former births. He said, I am the Vaishnavi Valmiki. I have become an avatar in this world to sing with my lips the story of Ram, and that I may turn men to devotion to Him. I was entangled in the enjoyment of temporary sensual joys. With this change of heart he came to Anandvan (Banaras). After taking bath in Bhagirthi he adopted severe austerities. He rejected cooked food and fruits and lived on the fallen leaves[7].

Another author has related about the marriage of Tulsidas that according to a widespread tradition, much of which is based on the Bhakta Mala, Tulsidas was married to the daughter of Dinabandhu Pathak called Ratnavali, and the couple's only son, Taraka, died in infancy.

The story goes that one day, Ratnavali decided to visit her father. Unable to bear the pain of separation, Tulsidas hurriedly caught up with her, only to hear her disapproving words to the effect that no one but Rama deserved such devotion and attachment.

> Are you not ashamed of following me here?
> A curse on such love !
> What can I say to you, my husband?

My body is nothing but bone and skin;
and if such love you have for it
had been devoted to the Lord Rama,
You would have no reason to dread rebirth.

The reprimand had such a profound effect on the poet that he abandoned his family ties shortly after, and returned to Banaras, where he became an ascetic votary to Rama.

It seems clear that the author of the Ramcharitmanas was reared from childhood in the cult of Rama, whose glory he sang until his death. It also seems clear that his rifaciment of the Ramayana won him immediate recognition, thus prompting Tulsidas admirers to liken him during his lifetime to Valmiki himself[8].

The renunciation of Tulsidas was in his day and in the context of his own life as decisive as that of the other Indian saints and sages from Gautam Buddha to Vivekanand who left hearth and home, not to find a way of escape but to search for the truth and share their knowledge with their fellow-men. Tulsidas, in any case, had no respect for those who turned sanyasis because they had "rost a wife or the family income had dwindled". His mind was ripe for the great decision and it would appear that his marriage and family life were just an interlude in a pilgrims progress towards spiritual self-realisation. The years in the life of Tulsidas that followed his renunciation of home and family were some of the most fruitful in developing his personality and outlook on life. It was during these years that he travelled up and down the country, gathering knowledge, studying men and affairs, meeting saints and sadhus and dwelling in meditation in a final bid to apprehend the Reality behind the apparent contradictions and disappointments of life. Unfortunately it is also a more or less dark period as far as dates and details are concerned. The places where he spent most of his time were Prayag, Ayodhya, Chitrakut and Kashi but he visited many other places far and near which find mention in his writings.

The place to which he naturally turned for solace, once he made up his mind to renounce the life of a householder, was

Ayodhya. There were many cultural and spiritual associations due to which the place was enshrined in his heart. It was Ram's own city and very much his own spiritual "home". It was near here that he had found refuge as a hapless and poverty-stricken child[9]. But the idea uppermost in his mind at the moment seems to have been to travel to the great pilgrim centres of the country, such as Jagannath Puri, Rameshwaram, Dwaravati, Badrikashram and the heights of the Himalayas. Apart from tradition and the accounts of these travels in the Mool Gosain Charit, there are very vivid descriptions of some of these places in his own writings. In a striking passage in the Vinaya Patrika, while praying Nar-Narayan he recalls the forests and mountain peaks of Badrikashram, the trials and hazards which the pilgrim has to face, the murderous attacks of armed robbers on the way and adds characteristically. "Lord, the journey of the spiritual seeker is nct less difficult. Poor Tulsidas is equipped neither with the supporting staff of true renunciation, nor the traveller's money of a firm grounding in dharma".

His description in the Ram Charit Manas of Mansrover in the Himalaya is equally alive with the warmth of feeling and it is not inconceivable that he had seen personally the blue mountain peaks and the jewelled stairs and transparent waters of the lake. The view certainly had enhanted his heart and was very much in his mind in choosing a title for his great epic.

There could no doubt that Tulsidas was a ceasters traveller in his youth and middle age and that was Ayodhya as his headquarters he visited many places, big and small, in northern India. References to these visits occur in his own works and in the works of contemporary writers. Places in Bihar and Uttarpradesh which had anything to do with the story of Shri Ram had naturally the strongest attraction for him. He used to stay at Prayag on the occasion of Makar Sankranti generally falls in the month of January every year. He used to move to Chitrakut during the month of February and March. In the month of April he used to remain in Ayodhya due to the occasion of Shri Ram's Birthday. From Ayodhya he would proceed to Kashi. After the rainy season he would go to Mithila because it would be the part of the year when his Lord Ram's wedding ceremony took place there.

It was very clear that during these travels he must have gathered a great deal of knowledge about men and affairs and with his keen, observant mind studied the manners and ways of living of various people to whom he met. Describing the banyan tree in the hermitage of the sage Valmiki at Sitamarhi (between Prayag and Kashi), he narrates, "Even an ordinary banyan tree is dwelt in by God Siva but the place is twice blessed because mother Sita lived in exile here at this spot and the sage Valmiki set up his hermitage. It is said that the people of this area are very soft spoken, polite and obliging.[10]

Another author has narrated the accounts of Tulsi's travel in these words:

From Prayag, Tulsi went to Ayodhya where he remained for four months during the rainy season. He then proceeded to the sacred city of Jagannath Puri on the east coast, where he arrived after twenty five halts on the way. From Puri he went southward to the island temple of Rameshwar, encircled by the way of Bengal and the Indian Ocean, where Shri Ram himself had installed an image of Siva. Afterwards he reached Dwarka on the west coast—a historical place full of the memories of Shri Krishna. There after he reached at the temple of Badri Narayan, hidden in the snowy peaks of the Himalayan range. This completed the four main pilgrimages, the fulfilment of which is even now the dream and aspiration of all pious Hindus. From Badri he went to the lake Mansrovar, in western Tibet. After staying there for a few days, he visited the Nilacala and Rupacala peaks, returned to Mansrovar and after walking reverently round the holy mountain of Kailas, came to Bhavabana where he remained during the monsoon. It stated in Mula Gosain Charita, that this pilgrimage lasted in all 14 years, 10 months and 17 days[11].

It happened one day that Tulsidas went into the forest to relieve himself. The water that remained in his vessel he poured upon the roots of the tree. Suddenly he noticed a most terrifying demon His two hands were joined together as he stood before Tulsidas. He said to Tulsidas, I am pleased with you. Whatever blessing you may ask, I will give it you. Tulsidas said to himself, Tell me who you are and why you have become pleased with me? I do not understand why? He replied, that I am a demon. I have been here for a long time. I drink the water which you pour on the roots. We have no permission to drink water from wells, tanks, rivers, or the sea, so I am very thirsty. You have supplied me with water for these twelve years. I will give whatever you ask for. Tulsidas with an astonished mind, said to himself, I was wishing for a visible manifestation of Shri Ram. The result of that desire has been the favour of this ghost. I planted a mango tree, and bore the fruit of the Vrindavan tree. So the performance of these austerities have brought me the favour of this ghost. I was wishing for a wishcow. Instead of her a pig appeared. So failing a manifestation of Shri Ram it is this ghost who is showing this favour to me. Having made a ring of sugar around a tree, there sprung out of it a bitter squash. So although my austerities have been good. It is this ghost who is pleased with me I was looking at a beautiful royal swan coming towards me, when suddenly I saw a crow instead. So instead of meeting Shri Ram it is this ghost that is pleased with me. It is like looking for association with the good, and then seeing a reviler coming forward. So instead of meeting the Husband of Janki, this has become pleased with me. While seeking philosophic knowledge, sensual stories may fall on one's ears. - so on and so far. Tulsidas said to him, ' You have become pleased with me, you say. I have no further desire in my heart than that you should help me to meet Shri Ram. As the name of Ram was heard by the demon he stepped back and said, If I should repeat His name by my lips it will mean my destruction. If you really wish to meet Him, Maruti is His servant. I can cause him to manifest himself to you. Tulsidas replied, "Where is Maruti? Show him to me at once. He will fulfil my desire". The demon answered, 'You are constantly listening to the Puranas. An aged Brahman is accustomed to come there. It is he who is Maruti. If you ask who he is I will tell you how he may be recognised. He comes and sits before anyone else. He leaves after every one has gone. He has a staff in his hand and a cap on his head. He wears an old garment and a loin cloth. If you see a form like that, you will know that he is the head of the monkeys. Thus speaking the demon became invisible, and Tulsidas returned to his hermitage. The next day after taking his bath, and repeating God's name as usual, he hastened to go where the Puranas was being read. When suddenly an aged Brahman appeared and seated himself there. Tulsidas saw that his appearance was just as described by the demon. When the recitation of the Purana was over, and all the listeners had gone, the aged Brahman in silence started to go. Tulsidas followed alongwith him. When he got outside the city, Hanuman (Maruti) was going very rapidly. Seeing himself all alone with him, he held the Brahman by his feet and said to him, 'Swami have compassion on me, Thou Mighty One'. The Brahman said to him, "Hallo who are you? Why have you held my feet ? I am a poor helpless lonely one". Tulsidas replied to him. You are Maruti, the bhakta of Shri Ram. Thus speaking he again fell at his feet. Maruti thought to himself, He is the muni Valmiki who has desconded as an avatar. He at once gave him an embrace, thus expressing his love. Maruti said to Tulsidas, 'I am pleased with you'. The other replied, My mind desires a gift by your favour. I want you so to act that I may have a manifestation of Shri Ram'. Saying I will do so, he (Hanuman) became invisible. Maruti said to Shri Ram, 'Listen to this my request. The bhakta Tulsidas is a full avatar of Valmiki. I want you to give him a visible manifestation of yourself. This is my desire, so fulfil the wish to my heart, O Swami', Hearing Maruti's words Shri Ram replied, 'I will do so'. So he called together all the monkeys and took the army with him. The Holder of the bow (Ram) passed in front of the hermitage of Tulsidas, but he did not recognise Him. He said to himself, ' Some ...Muhammadans are passing by. The monkeys seemed heroic and Shri Ram seemed to be the king of the Muhammadans. Seeing them thus, Tulsidas made them a namaskar. After that Maruti came to the hermitage of Tulsidas and said to him, 'Shri Ram has fulfilled your desire'. The other replied O Maruti, I have not met Shri Ram. 'Maruti replied why? He has just passed by your hermitage was truly a Muhammadan. I did not see Shri Ram. My desire still remains unfulfilled'. Maruti remarked, 'A wish-cow came to your house, and you wise fellow drove it away, thinking it was a goat. As you were once walking along the road you suddenly saw a touchstone, how is it that you, a wiseman, should throw it away thinking it was a mere pebbli? A very wise clever parrot happened to come to your hermitage. It seemed to you to be a dove, therefore you did not care for it. Mahipati quoted so many examples like this..... The Dweller in Ayodhya, the life of Janki was holding his bow and arrow in the same way as Valmiki described Him. Show me that appearances. When Maruti heard him say this, he smiled and said, Shri Ram will fulfil the desire of your heart. Saying this, Maruti became invisible and bringing the image of Shri Ram into his imagination he began his loving praise. 'Victory, Victory O Dweller in Ayodhya, Husband of Sita, Slayer of Ravan, Holder of the bow, Purifier of the sinner, Saviour of the humble, Slayer of demons, O Shri Ram'. Shri Ram replied, 'Maruti' why this special praise today? What is the special desire of your heart, that you have begun this loving praise? Maruti replied 'Shri Ram, wish tree of the desires of the bhaktas, Thou a visible form, dark as thick cloud. I desire Thee to visit Tulsidas. Hearing Maruti's request Shri Ram said, 'How can he have a direct manifestation in this Kali Yuga'? Maruti replied, 'O Lord of heart, he is an avatar of the rishi Valmiki. It was Thou who gavest the command that he should turn men to Thy worship. Hearing this remark of Maruti's Shri Ram said, 'I will listen to your request. I never break my word'. So Shri Ram with Sita and Lakshman, taking the form of visible avatars, walked alongwith Maruti. The bhakta Maruti went forward and informed Tulsidas. Said he, Shri Ram will today fulfil your hearts desire. Hearing Marutis remarks Tulsidas was full of joy. Just than he saw before him the Lord of Ayodhya. His joy now was without limit. A brilliant crown adored his head. He bore a yellow garment. This complexion was that of a dark cloud. In his hand was a bow and arrow. In this form he saw Shir Ram. With deep reverences Tulsidas bowed prostrals on the ground. And the merciful Shri Ram embraced his bhakta Tulsidas. Maruti said to him, 'you are a very fortunate man. WIth your eyes you have seen the form of Shri Ram. You must now proclaim to all men God's deads which you formerly described. In this Kaliyuga and means of salvation are not yoga practices, nor sacrifices, nor the study of Vedas. So proclaim the might of the God's names and turn men to the worship of God. Maruti said to Shri Ram, 'Place your hand on his head. Shri Ram listned to his request and gave Tulsidas the blessing of his assurance, and after that Shri Ram disappeared.

Chandra Kumari Handoo has narrated this incident as under:

In the forest named Bhava, Tulsi recited the Ramayana daily. A very interesting anecdate of this period is related by Babaji, and is also widely current in the traditional and other accounts of the life of Tulsi. We shall repeat it also. The spirit of a dead man, bound to a holy fig (Pipal) tree for some evil deeds of its past life, was suffering in great agony. Tulsi passed that way daily and poured water at the root of the tree after his morning ablution. This released the spirit from its painful bondage. Wishing to express its gratitude, the spirit asked Tulsi how the latter's kindness to a departed soul could be repaid. Tulsidas said he did not desire anything except the vision of Rama. The spirit replied that such a thing was completely beyond its power, but it knew the means by which this wish could be fulfilled. The spirit then informed Tulsi that when he recited the Rama Katha, Hanuman came to listen to him in the guise of a leper dressed in rags. Shunned by the audience, he sat in a corner and was the first to come and the last to go. The spirit said that Hanuman, by the strength of his own devotion could confer the boon of the vision (darsana) of Rama upon Tulsi. Next day, at the recital Tulsi looked carefully and found a man who answered to the description given by the spirit. When the assembled crowd of devotees had dispersed and this man was also about to leave. Tulsi went upto him, felt at his feet and begged him to fulfil the desire so dear to his heart. In vain the leper protested, but Tulsidas clung to his feet and implored him over and over again to be kind. At last he said ' Go to Chitrakut and there you will be blessed with the vision of Rama. Tulsi left the place immediately. Throughout the journey his mind dwelt on Rama and on the possibility of Rama darshan. Looking back to his life, he despaired at his own worthlessness, but his heart filled with hope and his steps became buoyant when he thought of the grace of Rama, which is never satisfied even by its own compassion.

On reaching Chitrakut, he lived at Ramghat and, following his usual routine of life, started his daily recitation of the Ramayana. One day while doing circumambulation (pradaksina) of Kamadagiri hill, Tulsi came across a most unexpected sight. Two princely looking boys of fair and dark complexion passed by riding on horses as if they were out on a hunting expedition. Attracted greatly for their extraordinary good looks he wondered who they were. It did not occur to him for a moment that they were Rama and Lakshmana, the ideals enshrined in his own heart, until Hanumanji enlightened him.

According to another version quoted by Sir George Grierson, Tulsi saw the two brothers with Sita and Hanuman returning to Ayodhya after the defeat and death of Ravana and the crowning of Vibhisana as king of Lanka. Tulsidas first mistook this vision for a scene from the pageant of Rama's life (Ramlila), but when he discovered his mistake he wept inconsolably. Hanuman pacified him in a dream and said that he had been the recipient of great grace, and no man or woman in the age of Kal Yuga could expect more. Instead of weeping over it Hanuman told Tulsi to prepare himself for serving him.

Of the two visions related above Babaji (Baba Ben i Madhav Das) confirms the earlier. According to him, Hanuman promised Tulsi that he would have another vision of Rama the next day. So, with the break of dawn, Tulsi went to Ramghat and busied himself in making sandalwood paste for the mendicants and pilgrims who had come for a bath in the holy Mandakini river. It was the sacred day of Mauni Amavasya, which fell on a Wednesday in Samwat 1607 (A.D. 1550), and a large number of people had assembled there for a bath and worship. Just at the time when everyone was busy, Rama suddenly appeared before Tulsi and said, 'Baba', give me some paste. Fearing that Tulsi might allow this golden opportunity to pass unheeded once again, Hanuman in the form of a parrot cried out to him from a neighbouring tree:

चित्रकूट के घाट पै भई संतन की भीर।
तुलसीदास चन्दन घिंसे, तिलक देत रघुवीर।।

The ghat of Chitrakut was crowded with holy men.!
Tulsidas rubbed the sandal wood and Rama anointed himself."

Tulsi looked up in surprise and saw the enchanting form of Rama standing in front of him. The currents and cross currents of random thoughts and desires were stilled in his heart, and as the consciousness of the world and the physical self slowly receded, his mind merged in Him completely. Rama again asked for the paste, but Tulsi was unable to move or speak. The Lord then bent down and with his own hand took a little of the sandalwood, put it on his forehead and disappeared[12]. Tulsi was in a deep trance, oblivious of his surroundings, when Hanuman again came to his rescue. Slowly he recovered, but was unable to return to ordinary consciousness till the night. This was the first time Tulsidas experienced samadhi[13].

The above quoted episode seems more authenticated that this has been narrated in the same fashion in the following words in *Ramcharitmanas*:

"On reaching Chitrakut, he lived at Ramghat. One day he set out for circumambulation (Parikarma) where he happened to have a glimpse of Shri Ram. He noticed that two most beautiful looking boys riding on horses alongwith bows and arrows were going that side. On seeing them Tulsidasji was much impressed, but failed to recognise them. Afterwards Hanumanji apprised him of the facts. Knowing this he repented a lot. Hanumanji pacified and assured him that early morning you will again have 'darshan' of Lord Shri Ram".

On the occasion of 'Mauni Amavasya', Wednesday during Samwat 1607 Shri Ram again appeared before Tulsidasji. In the guise of a child he requested Tulsidasji "Baba" please give me chandan paste. Hanumanji thought, that he may not be deceived, in the guise of parrot he narrated the following couplet:

चित्रकूट के घाट पै भई संतन की भीर।
तुलसीदास चन्दन घिंसे, तिलक देत रघुवीर।।

Seeing the most unexpected sight Tulsidasji was so overwhelmed and overjoyed that he became unconscious. Lord Rama with his own hands took chandan paste marked on His and Tulsidasji's forehead.... and disappeared.

During Samwat 1628 on the advice of Hanumanji he proceeded towards Ayodhya. These were the days of Magh Mela in Prayag. He stayed there for few days. After six days of the festival under a Banyan tree he happened to meet sage Bhardwaj and Yagyavalak. At that time the same story from Ramayan was being recited which he had listened from his Guru at Suker Kshetra. From there he went to Kashi and stayed in a Brahman's house at Prahlad ghat. During his stay at Prahlad ghat he was blessed by Mother Saraswati and enabled him to compile poetry couplet in Sanskrit. But astonishingly whatsoever he wrote during day time vanish at night. This happened daily on eighth day he saw a dream. He was advised by Lord Siva whatsoever you want to compile, write in your own language; seeing this he woke up. At the very moment Lord Siva and Parvati appeared before him. Tulsidas laid down and touched their feet. Lord Siva told him to go Ayodhya and stay there and take down your poetry in Hindi only. Due to my blessing your poetry will flourish like Samved. After saying so Lord Siva and Parvati disappeared. As per his Lords wish and advice Tulsidasji reached Ayodhya from Kashi.

Writing of the Ramcharitmanas

It was the beginning of Samvat 1633. That year on the auspicious occasion of Ramnaumi the stars were in the same Nakshatra (direction) as were in the Treeta Yug. Early in the morning Tulsidasji started writing Shri Ram Charitmanas. It was completed in two years, seven months and 26 days. During Samvat 1633 in the month of Margasirsa Shukla Paksh Nakshatra on the auspicious day of the marriage day of Shri Ram all the seven parts (Kands) were completed[14].

More details have been given by Beni Madhav Das in his book Mula Gosain Carita and also quoted by Chandra Kumari Handoo in her book. Tulsidas that in obedience to the wishes of

Hanumanji, Tulsidas left Chitrakut and reached Prayag. He reached there on the occasion of Magha Mela during the month of January, six days after the Makara Sankranti, Tulsidas saw two sadhus of dynamic personality under the banyan tree reciting the Ramkatha. He was surprised to note that the same story which he happened to listen at Sukar Khet was being recited here. One of the sages explained to him that Lord Siva first told the history of Shri Ram to Mother Parvati, then to Kaka Bhusundi who related the same to Yajana valkya, who was now reciting it to Bhardwaj. In these circumstances Tulsidasji once again heard the Ramkatha of his childhood days. But to his utter surprise when he went there the next day, the hut, the holy banyan tree and both the sages had all disappeared and were no where to be found. After this incident Tulsidas reached Banaras to pay his respects to Lord Siva, and then proceeded to Ayodhya. Walking in this manner, he reached Sitamadhi, where Rishi Valmiki Ashram was situated in ancient times. It is said that reaching there when Tulsidasji sat in meditation then he felt a radical change in his mind and the memories of Tulsidas life as Rishi Valmiki were awakened in Sitamadhi. For three days and nights Tulsidasji sat under the sacred banyan tree known as the Sita bata[15]. In Kavitavali Tulsidas has written in praise of Sitamadhi that the place where Valmiki the hunter, instructed by the seven sages, "mara-mara" (मरा मरा) and became a great saint. Being also the abode of Sita and the birth place of Lava and Kusa, Tulsidas says, the heat of the body is cooled by the shadow of this hermitage. By the banks of the Ganga stands the Sita-bata (a stately banyan and a king amongst trees); sinners are purified by its very sight. This land, bearing the impression of Sita's lotus feet lies between the villages of Baripur and Digpur[16].

There is a story about the background of Rishi Valmiki, that formerly he was an unregenerate hunter of wild animals, also earned a living by robbing and sometimes even by killing lonely travellers. Having once met the Seven sages, he repented of his misdeeds, but unable to utter the holy word Rama could only say mara-mara (मरा मरा) (by placing the two syllables of Rama in reverse order). He repeated word mara mara for many years with full faith and humility until, purified, he was chosen by the gods to write the life of Lord Rama. It is also said that Lava and Kusa, twin sons of Rama and Sita were also born in the Ashram of Valmiki[17]. Quoting from Mula Gosain Charit Handoo goes on to state that from Sitamadhi Rambhakat Tulsidasji went to Kashi and stayed with a pious brahmin. There a keen desire to sing the glory of Shri Rama arose in his heart, but whatever he composed in Sanskrit verse during the day he would forget overnight. This went on for several days and Tulsidasji wondered on such happenings. On the eighth day, however Lord Siva appeared to him in a dream and said 'Compose in your own spoken language'. These words were still echoing in Tulsi's ears when on waking, he had a vision of Siva and Parvati. Repeating the words of his dream, Lord Siva said 'Compose your verses in Hindi, my son. Do not get involved in the language of the gods i.e. (Sanskrit). You should do that which will be benefit to all, do not follow the traditional path. Go and live in Ayodhya and let your poetry come to light there. Through the grace of my meritorious deeds, your poetic talent will be as fruitful as the hymns of the Samaveda. Saying this, both the divine forms disappeared.

Early in the new Samvat year of 1631 (March-April) (A.D. 1574) the position of the planets and other astrological signs not excluding the day of the week, Tuesday, on Rama-Navami, the birthday of Bhagwan Ram, were exactly as they had been when Rama was born in the distant age of Treta. On this very auspicious day, Hanuman appeared, performed the purification ceremony (abhiseka) by the sprinkling of sacred water and chanting of mantars and installed him in a new life. Celestial beings such as Siva, Parvati, Ganesa, Sarasvati, Narada, Sesa, Surya, Sukracharya and Brihaspati also showered their blessings on him. And then at last Tulsidasji started his writing on the Ramcharitmanas. He wrote in all for 2 years, 7 months and 26 days, and was able to finish the book on a Tuesday afternoon, on the anniversary of the marriage of Shri Rama and Sita in the month of November-December (Margasirsa) of the Samwat year 1631 (A.D. 1574). According to Beni Madhav Das Tulsidasji was at that time seventy seven years of age[19].

The most important work of the 16th century, however, is

the classic Ramcharitmanas, popularly known as Tulsidas's Ramayana. The book, which has immortalised Tulsidas, became so popular that Tulsidas came to be hailed as a great sage. According to legends, Mirabai sent him letters for advice, Keshavdas called on him. Abdur Rahim Khan-i-Khan befriended him and accepted his recommendations to bestow favours on others. Raja Man Singh and Raja Todar Mal waited on him. During Akbar's time (1556-1605 A.D.) he was given grants of tax-free lands, which his disciples descendants continued to enjoy for generations. And there is a reference that he was once sounded for the grant of a Mansabdari, which he declined. For, he said he needed no temporal honours; the greatest honour was the one bestowed by the people. And they hailed him as a sage.

The popularity of Tulsidas roused hostility in the priestly classes who eked out a living on the basis of their knowledge of Sanskrit. He was harassed, and shuttled between Ayodhya and Kashi. The first two sections (cantos) of Ramcharitmanas were written in Ayodhya, whence he had to flee and the remaining cantos at Kashi, the city of Siva. Here too he was harassed.

According to the disciples of Tulsidas, there was great opposition by the Brahmins of Kashi to his attempt to propagate the great story of Shri Ram in the spoken language of the people. Despite the blessings of the greatest scholar of the age, Madhusudan Saraswati and the respect shown to him by "Rahim", Raja Man Singh and Raja Todar Mal, they threatened him with dire consequences. When opposition mounted, he had to shift his residence from one place to another (i.e. from Gopal Mandir to Assi Ghat). Attempts were now made to steal the book. Indeed he was advised to throw it into the Ganga. He resisted all attempts to threaten him and left it in the custody of one of his Bhumihar patron, Todar Mal, chief of the four villages that constitute the large part of Banaras today. Yet the threat of dire consequences continued.

Tulsidas must have been depressed because he appealed to his great monkey god Hanuman, for help. When Hanuman advised that he should write a petition to Shri Rama. Tulsi Das wrote Vinaya Patrika, wherein he refers to his humble beginnings from which Rama had rescued him and taken him into his protective care.

Tulsidas prays: "Lord, you full of compassion, and I seek your indulgence. I am the alms-man and you are the alms giver. I am a well know sinner, and you are the destroyer of sin. You are the lord and master of all those who have none to protect them. Where then stands an orphan like me? There is non more miserable than I, and none who saves men from miseries as you do. You are the Supreme Reality and I am, a mere soul. You are the master, I am the servant. You are my father, mother, friend and guru, a well wisher at all stages. Many indeed are the bonds of relationship between you and me. You may treat me as you wish to. All that I, Tulsi ask of you is to redeem me in the manner it is possible.

Tulsidas had a large circle of admirers and close friends who attended the daily congratulations of devotees of the Lord. These according to Gautamchandrika, included people from all walks of Life—Brahmins, Rajputs, ploughmen, labourers, sportsmen, musicians, poets, traders, weavers, betel-sellers, barbers and minstrels. In addition came large crowds from far and near. This too irked the priestly classes of Kashi. One day they rushed to Assi Ghat, where Todar Mal and Tulsidas stayed, with the intention of putting Tulsidas to death. But Tulsidas was not there. Challenged by Todar Mal, they killed him. Tulsidas who returned later to find his friend and patron dead, wept bitterly. A few years later in (1612) there was a dispute over the assets of Todar Mal between one of his two sons and the latters nephew. Tulsidas, who was approached, helped the dispute and the deed (in Persian) called "Panchayatnama", now in Maharaja Ramnagar's Library, is possibly the only document which has two verses in Hindi in Tulsidas's own hand.

Tulsidas who had been a witness to a few famines in Akbar's reign (1556-1605 A.D.) and later in Jahangir's time (1605-1626) A.D. and had been exploitation and misery of people, now, in the evening of his life, saw the sufferings of the people of Banaras afflicted by plague. He tended the poor. Later, he himself got pains all over his body and also suffered from boils. He appealed to Shri Rama to get rid him of his pains[20].

In a book entitled 'Singer Saints of India' Rajinder Singh Verma stated that Tulsidas declined a heavy purse offered to him by Jahangir (1606-1626)[21].

It will not be out of place to mention here that when Tulsidas was in Banaras all the inhabitants of Banaras listened to his services in the praise of God, and they built a hermitage for Tulsidas. There were wealthy and pious men to whom Tulsidas gave his mantar and made them his disciples. They used to bring a variety of things and place them in the hermitage. A thousand Brahmans daily dined along with Tulsidas. Any poor person, any beggar, anyone without food if he came there, went away satisfied. His reputation became great among the people. The brought for him unlimited amounts of money, great, great olden plates and an unlimited and innumerable amount of silver. But Tulsidas was untouched by them. He had neither joy nor sorrow. After the feast of the Brahmans, there followed the enthusiasm of the praise-service. Pious people came in large numbers in order to repeat God's names. People left their doors open while all went to sleep. Thus they thought of the feet of Shri Ram, when dreaming and in dreamless sleep and when awake. Two thieves therefore considered the situation carefully. We see no one in the hermitage of Tulsidas who would refuse us admission. We can go there without fear, and take away a load of golden plates. We can take away as much as our hands are able to carry. After the praise service of God was overall the audience went to sleep. Just then two thieves came and began to steel. They gathered up the golden plates with their hands and tied them up in a bundle. They placed the load on their heads and started to leave hurriedly. As they came near the gate they found two men seated therewith bows and arrows, very stout lookingmen. The astonished mind of the thieves said to them 'A while ago there was no sentinel here to protect the place. So they turned back quickly and arrived at the northern gate. They suddenly saw a person with shining contenance with a crown and ornaments. In his hand were a bow and arrow. The thieves saw him from afar and became ashamed. Then they went to the south door, but there also sat the door keeper. The thieves thought this very strange and came back and sat down. The two thieves thought to themselves. "These men holding the bow will soon get up and go away. Then we will quickly take away these golden plates. Thus remarking to one another, the thieves sat quickly for four ghatikas and then they went to the gate and looked. And there they saw the two men seated with bow and arrows in their hands, with the string drawn to their ears, and standing in a position to shoot. The thieves became frightened, threw down the gold plates and went to the gate, but they were not allowed to pass. The night passed in great anxiety of mind. The sun now arose, and all the bhaktas arose when the wicks were lighted for waving. After the early morning repetition of God's names, Tulsidas came out of his hermitage . Just them the two thieves came and fell at his feet. The thieves filled with emotion said to him, For give us our fault. Tulsidas said to them, in reply "Tell me who you are? They replied, ' we are thieves, who had come to rob you. But there were soldiers of the bow seated at the gate and they would not let us pass. We had made a bundle of your golden plates and were waiting in your hermitage. It was a great fault on our part, forgive us, you merciful one. Being a bhakta of Shri Ram, you are, supremely generous. At night you leave your door open. Therefore we came in without fear. Tulsidasji had many disciples. He therefore asked them who is at the gate protecting us ? Why have you placed them there without my knowledge. I have already told you that it was alike to me whether anyone gave to me or took away. Worship Shri Ram with love. The disciples replied with an oath. We swear by your feet that we do not know who is guarding the door. The thieves replied, His face was brilliant. He wore a crown and ornaments. He was dressed in a yellow robe. His complexion was dark. He is seated there even now. All were astonished, and coming near to the gate they looked, but they saw nothing and thought this very strange. Tulsidas started weeping. He said to himself 'Shri Ram and Lakshman have now become my doorkeepers at this time. Tulsidas who could not obtain by adopting the severest postures in yoga practices visits to various sacred places would not give him got at his door steps 'Shri Ram' the dweller in Ayodhya as a doorkeeper .... Tulsidas then said to the thieves, 'whatever you want to take, take it away to your homes. Do not feel shy. After hearing these words from Tulsidas, the thieves fell at his feet. They cried out 'Have mercy on us and place your assuring hand upon us. We are sinful, evil men. We were encircled by ignorance, but by the power of association with you, we have seen a manifestation of Shri Ram. Tulsidas said to them, 'Your good fortune is very great. Without any efforts on your part, Shri Ram gave you a manifestation of Himself. Hearing him say this, the thieves made him a namaskar and putting aside their evil minds, constantly remained in Tulsidas hermitage[22].

Mahipati has quoted another miracle of Tulsidas in his writing that one day a few Brahmanas were taking food in the hermitage of Tulsidasji. When Tulsidasji was about to make the offering to the gods, and as the Brahmans were repeating the words, This is an offering to the Supreme Brahma, suddenly a Brahman appeared at the gate, listen to what he said. First repeating the names of Sita and Ram, he said 'I am a great killer of Brahmans, give me some of the food you give to those who ask for it. This was what he said. When the Brahmans who were present heard him, they were all filled with wonder. Tulsidas came outside and embraced him. He took the Brahman by the hand and seated him by his side. He then said to him, 'O Swamji, personification of mercy, listen to my request. The moment you utter the words Sita and Ram, sins like that of killing Brahmans and similar sins are burnt up. Afterwards Tulsidasji requested the Brahmans to start eating, but they did not acceded to his request instead questioned him that on what authority have you seated this Brahman killer in our line? Tulsidasji replied to them, 'there is one authority for it. How can the sin of killing a Brahman remain, when uttering the name of Ram? But the Brahmans were quite adamant and insisted that untill and unless you prove it we do not take any food?

He at once took a plate of food and went into the temple of Vishveshvar, the Lord of the Universe. All the Brahmans now arose and followed him. They stood in the assembly hall and all looked with curiosity. With the plate of food in his hand Tulsidas came to the great door of the temple. He joined his hands palm to palm, and bowed prostrate on the ground. Said he, 'Victory, victory to Thee who wearest the moon on Thy head blue throated one, Holder of the Khatvanga bow, Husband of Parvati, Enemy of the demon Tripur, listen to the request of the lowly one. Just as Thou did drink the virulent poison, and thy whole body became inflamed, then Thou repeat the names of Ram. By merely repeating the two lettered name of Ram became cool, O Lord of the universe. If that be true, then let this stone bull eat this offerings. As soon as the prayer was heard a very strange thing happened. The stone bull arose and began to breathe violently. After eating all the offerings he ate up the, whole leaf plate. Everybody witnessed this miracle. Blessed was that time and happy day. Having shown this miracle, the stone bull sat quietly... All the Brahmans standing around Tulsidas said, now we know that you are truly a full avatar of Valmiki.

Neither the Vedas nor the Shastras understand the most extraordinary power of a bhakta. The noble Vaishnavas all shouted out, 'Victory, Victory'. While repeating the names of God all the twice born made a namaskar to Tulsidasji. They said 'Blessed are you noble Vaishnava. You are very wise in the spheres of the knowledge of eternal truths. Now we know that you are truly a full avatar of Valmiki.

Just as the moon stands supreme among the clusters of stars,

Just as the eagle is supreme among..... birds,
Just as Vishnu is supreme among the .....Gods,
................so you are supreme among the Vaishnavas
Just as Shiva is supreme among the ascetics,
Just as muni Vyas is supreme among the Rishis,
Just as Mother Rukmini was supreme among the cow-herdesses,
.............so you are, supreme among the Vaishnavas.
as the Husband of Janaki is supreme among the Holder of bows,
as the ocean of milk is supreme among all oceans.
As the son of Anusuaya is supreme among those who had attained God head, so you are supreme among the Vaishnavas. As the fourth stage of deliverence among the four stages as the father of

Brahmadev among the Yadavas, as the expounder of the Vedas among Pandits, are each supreme, so you are supreme among bhaktas.

As the sun among the nine planets,
As the Ushana among the great poets,
As the mount Meru among mountains, are each supreme, so you are the noblest Vaishnava among the Vaishnavas.

Thus having praised Tulsidasji, all the Brahmans came back to the hermitage. They allowed the Brahman killer to sit at their side and all dined together. Thus all the people of Banaras began to repeat the names of God. They gave up their pride and came to listen to the deads of Hari.

Notes and References

Marriage and Renunciation

1. Shri Ramacharitmanas—Tulsidas.
2. Tulsidas—Chandra Kumari Handoo.
3. *Ibid.*
4. Mula Gosain Charita quoted by Handoo, p. 23.
5. *Ibid.*
6. Dohavali,p. 88,quoted by Handoo,p. 25.
7. The Life of Tulsidas—Translation of Mahipatis Marathi Bhaktavijaya by Dr. Justice E. Abot and Narhari R. Godbola.
8. Love of God and Social Duty in the Ramcharitmanas by Edmour J. Babineu—Motilal Banarsidas, Delhi, 1979, p. 15.
9. Tulsidas by Devendra Singh, p. 18.
10. Tulsidas—Chandrakumari Handoo, p. 29.
11. *Ibid.*
12. Mahipati's translation.
13. Manas/Mula Gosain Charita—quoted by Chandra Kumari Handoo, p. 30-31.
14. Shri Ramcharitmanas.

15. Tulsidas—Chandra Kumari Handoo.
16. Kavitavali by Tulsidas quoted by Handoo.
17. Tulsidas by Handoo.
18. *Ibid.*
19. *Ibid.*
20. Tulsi Das by Madan Gopal in an article in Ramayana, Mahabharata, and Bhagvata writers—Pub. Div.
21. Tulsidasa by Rajinder Singh Verma (Singer Saints of India).
22. Mahapatis translation—pp. 41-44.
23. *Ibid.*, p. 48-49.

3

Ramcharitmanasa and Intellectual of Kashi

After completing the writing of Shri Ramcharitamansa by the grace of God Tulsidasji reached Kashi. After reaching there Tulsidasji read out Ramcharitamansa to Lord Vishvanath and Mother Annpurna. At night the book was kept in the temple of Shri Vishvanath. Early in the morning when the gates of the temple were opened it was found written,"Satyam Shivam Sundram" and below this were the signature of Lord Siva. The people assembled on that occasion heared the sound of "Satyam Shivam Sundram".

When this news reached to the Pandits of Kashi they were jealous. They started criticising Tulsidasji and tried their level best to spoil the book. They sent to thieves to steel the book. Thieves noticed that Tulsidasji's hermitage is being guarded by brave young men with bow and arrows in their hands. Both were very handsome with a dark complexion. While seeing them there the minds of both the thieves were changed. They determined not to steal anything in future and decided to devote themselves in the service of God Almighty. After this incident Tulsidasji felt that Shri Ram has to take trouble every now and then for him, he immediately disposed off entire household's belonging and distributed it among the people and kept Shri Ramcharitamansa with his friend Todarmal's safe custody. After this he prepared another copy of Shri

Ramcharitamanas. Afterwards so many copies were prepared. The popularity of the book was increasing day by day.

The Pandits of Kashi were greatly upset. When they failed to reach any conclusion they requested the renowned scholar Shri Madhusudan Saraswati to look into the book. After going through the book he was fully impressed and pleased and expressed his opinion in the following words:

आनन्दकानने ह्यस्मिञ्जङ्गमस्तुलसीतरु।
कवितामञ्जरी भाति रामभ्रमर भूषिता।।

(In Kashi, the forest of joy,
Tulsi is a walking tulsi plant,
His poetic blossom is full of beauty
On it the bee of Rama is ever humming).

When the pandits came to enquire about Madhusudan's opinion about the book which he had already glanced, he told them, you should ask this question to Lord Shiva Himself, instead of putting this question to me about it. They took Shri Ramcharitmansa to the temple of Visvanatha, kept it in front of the image of Lord Visvanatha, and kept over it the Puranas, the Sastras and then the Vedas. The temple was closed at night; when it was opened in the morning, the offending book was found right on top, taking precedence even over the Vedas. The pandits have to cut a sorry figure. They saluted Tulsi, and begged for forgiveness and as a token of their repentence they humbly washed his feet and sprinkled the water from them in their homes to purify themselves.

Tulsidas started living at Asighat. On one night Kali Yug came to him and started frightening him. Goswami Tulsidas remembered Hanumanji. Hanumanji advise him to write down 'Vinayapatrika'. Then Tulsidasji as desired by Hanumanji took down Vinayapatrika and presented to Shri Ram. Shri Ramji put his signature on it and thus Tulsidas get rid of all the evil designs of Kali Yug[1].

Baba Beni Madhavdas has also related the above quoted incident in his book 'Gosain Charit'. But in the Ramcharitmanasa it is recorded that Tulsidasji first of all read out Shri Ramcharitmanasa to Lord Vishvanath and mother Anapurna. On the contrary Baba Madhavdas has written that the book was first read out in the presence of Pawanputra Hanuman who blessed Goswami Tulsidas in these words:

> May your name and fame spread in all the three worlds i.e. Akash, Parithvi and Patal. Shri Ruparuna Swami, of Mithila, who was a pious person was the second lucky man to hear it from Tulsidas. A disciple of Swami Nandalala named Dayaludasa made a copy of Shri Ramcharitmanas for himself and read it out for his Guru, most probably in Brindaban. Later on Rasakhan, a prominent Hindi poet and staunch devotee of Lord Krishna heard it. After few days as desired by Shri Ram Tulsidasji reached Kashi and in the temple of Shri Vishvanath recited Ramcharitmanas to the divine and invisible presence of Shiva and Parvati. As stated earlier that keeping in view of the Pandits of Kashi the book was kept near the image of Lord Shiva and the doors of the temples were closed. A large number of people crowded the gates of the temple in the morning eager for darshan. At the time of the opening of the temple gate the people were surprised to see and note that they found beautifully written Satyam, Shivam, Sundaram on the title of Shri Ramcharitmanasa, bearing signatuare of Lord Shiva Himself. The gathering not only saw this in black and white but they heard the sound of recitation of Satyam, Shivam, Sundram in the premises of the temple. This was a great miracle in the Kali Yug and news spread far and wide like wild fire. People flocked around Goswami Tulsidasji to have his darshan, blessings and to touch his feet.

Kashi being an ancient city and a known seat of Sanskrit learning and stronghold of Hindu orthodoxy from the ancient times, the pandits of Kanshi made a strong protest because they were of the firm opinion that God should be praised in 'devabhashi' i.e. Sanskrit only. But Tulsidasji effort of taking down the story of Shri Ram in the spoken language of the common people was well received and appreciated by innocent Indians. The narrowness of heart and prejudicial attitude of the local intelligensia and their spiritual pride completely blinded them and did not acknowledged the merits of Shri Ramcharitmanasa. They could not tolerate the growing popularity that they conspired to steal this pious book and engaged two thieves namely Nidhua and Sidhua. But God's will was otherwise. As stated earlier that when both the thieves tried to enter the hut of Goswami Tulsidasji at the dead of night they found two young chaps, one with a fair and the other of dark complexion going up and down, with bow and arrows in their hands, thus gaurding the hut of Tulsidasji. When both the thieves named Nidhua and Sidhua observed these beautiful young man having dynamic personality so vigilant throughout the whole night the minds of these hired persons automatically changed and decided not to do the assigned job. In the morning they approached Tulsidasji and enquired about the night watchmen. By knowing the description of both the young men Tulsidas started weeping bitterly and distributed all his belongings among the needy persons. Tulsidasji embraced and congratulated Nidhua and Sidhua on having darshan of Shri Ram and Lakshman. They fell at his feet and mended the ways of their lives. Thus the Pandits of Kashi failed in their mission to destroy Shri Ramcharitmanasa. This version of this incident seemed most authenticated as Baba Beni Madhav Das and other scholars have mentioned in their writings or commentary on Bhakal Mal and Ramcharitmanasa.

As this was the only hand written copy of Shri Ramcharitmanasa which was saved by the grace and blessing of Shri Ram, Tulsidasji took down another copy of Ramcharitmanas and more copies were prepared. For the proper safety of the book the original book was kept in the house of his friend namely Todar Mal.

After the failure of their first attempt to acquire Ramcharitmanasa through thieves the Pandits of Kashi were greatly upset. They have not acknowledged the greatness of the book by their heart but were still adamant to destroy the book. Now they approached some tantric to use his tantric knowledge of kill Tulsidasji. The tantric invoked the spirit of Bhairon Baba, who failed to harm Tulsidasji due to the timely help of Shri Hanuman. Instead Bhairo Baba killed that tantric. Disappointed from every where they complained Madhusudan Saraswati; the well known scholar of that time that Lord Shiva had signed Tulsi's Ramcharitmanasa but he failed to convince us that how he compares with the Vedas and Puranas. After going through the book he was fully satisfied and when

Pandits enquired from him of his comments, he said why don't you put the question to Lord Shiva Himself, instead asking me about it. Thus the authenticity of the book was proved and Pandits of Kashi saluted the greatness of Tulsidasji[2].

The Ramcharitmanasa which he finished within a few years of his coming over to Kashi is undoubtedly the work which brought the widest fame to Tulsidas and enjoyed the greatest popularity with his audience. But he lived for nearly half a century after he had finished it and the majority of his works other than Ramcharitmanas were written or collected after his reputation as the author of the immortal epic had been firmly established.

There is a long list of the works of Tulsidas but the consensus of opinion among scholars is that only twelve can be named as his own works with any degree of certainly. These twelve books are:

1. The Vairagya Sandipani
2. The Ramagya Prasna
3. The Ramlala Nahchhu
4. The Janaki Mangal
5. The Ramcharitmanas
6. The Parvati Mangal
7. The Krishna Gitavali
8. The Gitavali
9. The Vinaya Patrika
10. The Dohavali
11. The Barwai Ramayan and
12. The Kavitavali[3]

Babineau has given the list of following 14 books:

1. Ramlala Nahchhu undated but shows immaturities of style and of content.
2. Ramajna Prasna dated Samwat 1621 (A.D. 1564).
3. Jnanadipika dated Samwat 1621 (A.D. 1564) in a new manuscript recently came to light.
4. Vairagya Sandipani undataed, but reveals less talent than the Ramcharitmanasa.
5. Janaki Mangal undated, shows influence of the Adhyatma Ramayan.
6. Ramcharitmanasa dated Samwat 1631 (A.D. 1574).
7. Satsai dated Samwat 1642 (A.D. 1585).
8. Parvati Mangal dated Samwat 1643 (A.D. 1586).
9. Gitavali (also known as Padavali Ramayana) undated.
10. Krishna Gitavali undated, but written before A.D. 1605 for Ramu Dvivedi refers to it in his Prema Ramayana, which was written in that year; a collection of songs on Shri Krishna.
11. Vinaya Patrika
12. Kavitavali
13. Hanuman Bahuka
14. Dohavali.

Books serialised at no. 11-14 all are undated, but frequent references to Tulsidasji's ill health and to the pestilence of A.D. 1616 suggest the last twenty years of his life[4].

Regarding other writings of Goswami Tulsidasji Handoo has mentioned that during Samvat 1640 (A.D. 1583) Tulsidas collected the verses of the Dohavali into the form of a book. At that time he was in Kashi. Two years later on the occasion of Sita Navami i.e. the birthday of Sitaji he started the writing of the Satsai. The poet Rahim composed a poem in Barve metre and sent it to Tulsidas; in acknowledgement and appreciation of the same, the latter wrote his Barve Ramayana in the same metre. In Mithila Tulsi composed the Ramalala Nahchhu, Parvati Mangal, Janaki Mangal and Hanuman Bahuka during his illness and some time later the Vairagya Sandipani and Ramajna Prasna. He then revised all his smaller books. Being old and weak, he was unable to copy them out himself, so they were written at his dictation by other people. Handoo further adds that there is no mention of Tulsidas' book Kavitavali in Mula Gosain Charit. She assumed that poems written by him at different times were apparently collected after his death and was entitled Kavitavali or Kavita Ramayana by his followers[5].

Except in the case of a few, such as the Ramcharitmanasa, the Ramagya Prasna and the Parvati Mangal, the poet gives us no indication as to when a particular work was written. This is perhaps natural as a majority of the undated works are collections of verses written from time to time. Of the manuscript copies of Ramcharitmanasa now available, the oldest written in 1604, about twenty years before the poet's death, is the one preserved at Ayodhya. Another copy is preserved at Malihabad near Lucknow, the capital of modern Uttar Pradesh and it is a measure of the intrinsic qualities of the Manas that of the making of commentaries and translations of the great epic both in Indian and foreign languages there is no end.

Ram and the story of Ram remained the principal theme and fountain head of inspiration in all his major works but having written the great epic, the poet seems to have developed a pronounced tendency to express himself in song and lyric. The thin thread of the story of Ram by which the poems in a particular collection are sought to be held together often recedes in the back ground and the poets love of beauty, form, colour and music comes to the foreground.

The Gitavali relates the story of Ram in songs but there is no attempt either to develop the story or strike a balance among the various episodes. The charm of the songs consists in their naturalness, sincerity of emotion and musical quality. The poet deliberately chooses scenes and episodes which lend themselves to lyrical treatment. They have a charming pictorial quality and there is an intimate connection between the mood evoked and the musical raga in which they are cast. Tulsidas had evidently an interest in music and it is not unlikely, as tradition has it, that the poet wrote these songs for ardent young musicians who sung the glories of Ram before eager and devout audiences.

With all his preoccupation with matters of deep spiritual import, Tulsidas had a lively interest in the lives and fortunes of the men and women among whom he moved and in making them interested in the story of Ram. Three short but charming literary pieces, the Ramlala Nahchhu, the Parvati Mangal and the Janaki Mangal seem to have been specially written to please and interest the ladies.

Tham Ramlala Nahchhu is a book in twenty stanzas, describing the rites connected with the sacred thread and wedding ceremonies and recalls the auspicious occasion and joyous scenes in the king's palace at Ayodhya.

In the Parvati Mangal the poet describes the wedding of Shiva and Parvati. He had described the episode earlier in the Ramcharitmanasa but the Parvati Mangal as an independent literary work has a charm of its own. It is compact in form. The economy and simplicity of the style are striking, which is something of a triumph for an epic poet. For once we have the date 1586 when it was written long after he must have finished writing the Ramcharitmanasa. It certainly should have provided an effective answer to the allegations of those who said he had glorified Ram at the expense of Shiva.

There is a close resemblance between the Parvati Mangal and the Janaki Mangal both in style and theme. In the Janaki Mangal, the wedding of Ram and Janaki is described in 216 stanzas, full of warm feeling and sensuous beauty.

All the three works are written in the language of the people, pure Avadhi, and in the metre mainly of the wedding songs, Sohar, to recall scenes which would delight the ladies. This shows not only how much the poet cared for the common people but also how keenly he felt that good poetry could be written to record common experiences for the common people in their own language.

It is significant that Tulsidas has written in praise of Shri Krishna with as full throated ease as about Shiva and in strains quite as sincere as those of Surdas. The language of Shri Krishna Gitavali is Pure Braj, the language spoken in the region in Western Uttar Pradesh which was the scene of Shri Krishna's exploits. The poems in this collection of songs, sixty one in number, compare very favourable indeed with the best manner of the poems in the Sursagar of Surdas.

It would appear that Tulsidas made experiments in practically all the various literary forms that were extent and popular in his day and he touched nothing which he did not adorn. As a metrical form, the Doha had been used by a long line of Hindi poets and saints and Tulsidas himself had used it to great effect in his Ramcharitmanasa to sum up or finalise ideas in a set of preceding lines. He must have seen how fit a vehicle it was for expressing crisp and quotable truth or observation in a concentrated form. Naturally there is a great variety of subject-matter in the Dohavali of Tulsidas, which is a collection of verses written at various times. From the maturity insight and acuteness of observation in a very large number of them, however, it is natural to suppose that the collection was made at a comparatively advanced stage in the poet's literary carrier. Thirty-four dohas in a set known as 'Chatak-Chautisa in this collection are remarkable for the presentation of the poet's own ideal and philosophy of love, love which seeks neither reward nor recompense, love which is utterly and entirely selfless love which is an ever fixed marks which neither storm nor tempest can shake. There is also in the Dohavali a great deal of worldly wisdom based on close observation of trends in society, men and affairs.

Another metrical form which caught the fancy of the poet was the Barwai, which he used for writing yet another Ramayana, the Barwai-Ramayan. It is said that the original Barwai-Ramayan contained many more than the sixty-nine verses to be found in the editions now generally available. In any case, both the language which is pure Avadhi, and the metre, which was rarely used, except by Tulsidas's contemporary. Abdur Rahim Khan-i-Khana, had a special appeal for the poet. It is a metre delicately designed to make for economy of phrase and concentration of ideas, highly responsive to the evocation of the finer shades of feeling and gracefully languid in movement.

The wide appeal of Tulsidasji's language and style as a poet is due mainly to its simplicity, adequacy and directness. What does it matter, he would say, "whether one writes in Sanskrit or the language of the people? What matters above all is true love". He believed strongly that it was not words but the sincerity of feeling behind them that shaped a poet's language and style. His own language and style went through a process of steady evolution from the pure Avadhi of his lesser works to the refined and fully developed, composite language of his major works such as the Ramcharitmanasa, the Kavitavali and the Vinaya Patrika. It is a composite language in the sense that he uses with perfect case and freedom and without any inhibition words drawn not only from Avadhi, Bhojpuri, Bundeli, Brijbhasha and Khariboli but also from Sanskrit, Arabic and Persian. The flexibility of his language is amazing. It would seem that it varies with the subject matter in hand a fully developed and refined Avadhi in the Ramcharitmanas and the Barwai-Ramayan, a perfected Brijbhasha for the Krishna Gitavali, the Kavitavali and the Vinaya-Patrika, Sanskrit laden lines for prayers and invocations and words drawn from Persian and Arabic, if the context demands it. Nothing seems to weigh with him as much as the basic need for naturalness, directness and effectiveness. If in the process it is necessary to take liberties with the rulers laid down by the purists, he does not hesitate to do so in the larger interests of vitality, freshness and adequacy of expression. He is in this matter more the creator of a language and idiom of his own and an original craftman than the follower of set rules and static tradition. He may be a little fond of similes and metaphors but this is so not because he wants to show off but because he knows such devices will convice his readers.

The result is that he lives up to his promise he would write poetry which may not please the purists and the pedants but which would win the hearts of the masses because it is full of the love of Ram.

The Kavitavali gives us rich material both about Tulsidasji's own life and the life of the common man in the society of his time. Together with the Hanuman Bahuk, it contains 369 quatrains, mostly in Kavita and Savaiya metres. In the earlier part of the work, the poet gives some unforgetable word pictures of situations in the story of Ram is quatrains of exquisite, beauty, remarkable as much for the meaning as for the musical sound effects, the movement of the lines and the inherent lyricism. But by the time the concluding canto, the 'Uttar Kand', is reached, the story of Ram comes to an end, the poet for once begins to talk about himself, his early life and struggles, his rise to fame, his allegiance to Ram and the rest of the work is the story not of Ram but of Tulsidas himself. Reviewing life from the vantage-ground of old age, he records with arresting frankness and sincerity the articles of his faith. He feels that man is not alone, that a life in tune with Ram has infinite possibilities, that life's greatest fulfilment is to live in God, above the dualities of poverty and affluence.

A keen social conscience is also in evidence in many of these quatrains. The poet is moved by the sight of "Ravana of Poverty holding the world in his grip". He draws a graphic picture of people in dire distress asking one another. "Where shall we go? What shall we do?" Because the farmers have no fields to cultivate, the beggars get no alms, the businessman have no vocation, and servicemen seek jobs in vain. He observes that people in all ranks of society resort to questionable and immoral devices to keep body and soul together and arrives at the conclusion that "there are no fires more devastating than the fire of hunger". He is unhappy because people have given up the right path laid down by the Shastras and all sorts of new fangled beliefs hold the field. The misery-vice and poverty he saw all around him and the confusion created in men's minds by the so-called religious men seem to have persuaded him that there is no religion for man higher than the service of his fellow-men.

The Vinaya Patrika ranks only with the Ramcharitmanasa as one of the crowning glories of the works of Tulsidas. It is a collection of lyrical songs. In the epic, the poet had to express his love for Shri Ram through the speech and action of others and the purposes of successful characterisation and dramatisation had to be met first. The general reader could see the deeper aspects of the poet's message of love only as through a glass darkly. In the Vinaya Patrika, which is in a real sense a sort of a spiritual biography, the poet is face to face with his Maker. He gives here, with fascinating candour and great intensity of feeling, a record of his endeavours to discover Reality and the true nature of the way of Love. This has led to a widespread but mistaken belief that it is some sort of a philosophical treatise in verse. His intensely personal, intimate approach, sincerity of feeling and lyrical quality of the songs, make it one of the finest collections of devotional verses in all literature.

The story goes that when Kali found that the life and works of Tulsidas were weaning people away from him and making in roads on his own domains, he threatened the poet with dire consequences. The good god Hanuman advised the poet to present a petition in the court of Shri Ram. Both the title and the concluding verses of the collection lend colour to the story. But apart from the story, the feeling which inspires the poet, that he is laying bare his heart at the feet of his Master, helps both to organise the songs and to give them their unique devotional flavour. Each poem is a human record of the poet's struggle with the flesh and the devil, his attempts to solve the riddle of the universe, his eagerness to get into touch with the sources of light, peace and joy. And the conclusions he arrives at give us valuable hints both about his nature convictions and his inner personality. He finds that there is an all-pervading divinity" in the beginning, the middle and the end. To get into touch with it is the greatest opportunity of human life. Mere intellectual discussion is a little use here. It will not help a man to see light if he only sits enveloped in the darkness of a close room by night and talks endlessly about a lamp and its light. If man could conquer anger, greed and ignorance, he could see light. But it is not so easy to conquer them. Asceticism, austerities, elaborate rites and rituals are the ways suggested, but it is like making a rope of dust to bind down an elephant. Love, faith and surrender to the will of a Master who is full of compassion for the lowliest and the vilest are the only way.

The spontaneous feeling, the deep personal note, the unity and concentration of thought which we seek in the great lyric are all there in the songs of spiritual self surrender collected in the Vinaya Patrika. There is no other work in which the authentic voice of the poet is to be heard more directly and distinctly.

The calamities which overtook Kashi in his old age moved Tulsidas deeply. These were the famine and the great plague during the reign of the Mughal emperor, Jahangir (ruled India between 1605-1626 A.D.). Contemporary records have it that the plague broke out in Agra about the year 1616 but from the manner the poet associates the epidemic with an astrologically evil period called 'Meena ki Sanichari", it would appear that it visited Kashi even earlier. There is a note of deep misery over the plight of fellow citizens in the powerfully objective picture of the havoc caused which the poet has drawn. He prays to his gods to spare Kashi for the city of Shankar and turned into a city of the dead and the dying.

Tulsidas himself suffered from some particularly painful disease about this time, which has led some writers to make the conjecture that he was caught by the plague and that his death too could be traced back to its after effects. In the Hanuman Bahuk and elsewhere he does refer to his physical ailments and prays to his favourite deities to spare him. But there is nothing in these references which could help us to identify the disease or trace out the exact cause of his death. On the other hand, there are clear indications that at least once when he fell ill, he was saved through the good offices of his patron deity Hanuman. Another ailment of his he describes as a pain in the arms which spread to other parts of the body. This ailment seems to have given him no end of trouble and in a number of quatrains in the Hanuman Bahuk he states how he prayed to all the gods in turn and in the end became silent, realising that he "must reap what he had sown". This turning of the searchlight inwards is so characteristic of the poet that it would be very far fetched to conclude that because his prayers were not answered, he lost all faith in divine intervention, or that he died of the plague[6].

The Ramcharitmanasa is so popular that people recite it or hear it being recited. There is no village in Northern India where the story is not recited or staged every year at the time of Dussehra and its verses quoted by million of people ranging from the scholar to the innocent and illiterate villager. While listening people deeply moved. During recitation at several contexts, they shed tears. It is the Hindu ideal or the code of conduct. The popularity of this book has been unrivalled. What greater tribute to a writer could there be than the fact that the accepted form of greeting in Northern India is "Jai Ramji Ki".

Mahatma Gandhi, in his story of 'My Experiments with Truth' said, "What left a deep impression on me was the reading of Ramayana before my father... The reader was a great devotees of Rama — Ladha Maharaj of Bileswar... I must have been 13 years old at that time, but I quite remember being enraptured by his reading. That laid the foundation of my deep devotion to the Ramayana. Today, I regard to the Ramayana of Tulsidas as the greatest book of all devotional literature. Throughout Mahatma Gandhi's writings we find him profusely quote verses from Tulsidas, he new the whole work by heart and drew such inspiration from it that he is reported to have said that there was no situation in human life to which Tulsidas had not referred. When once a questioner asked him where from he drew inspiration for his non-cooperation movement, Gandhiji referred to the dialogue between Ravana, the demon king of Lanka, and Sita who had been given an ultimatum that she must respond to his overtures or face dire consequences. That is what Sita told Ravana: "Only two things can touch my neck. They are either the soft-but-as-strong as an elephant's-trunk-like arms of my husband Rama: or the sword. No third force can touch me". This, said Gandhiji always insisted that he drew inspiration from Tulsidas for his belief that Truth signifies God. And the ideal for which Gandhiji worked all his life was "Rama Rajya", the state of governance in Rama's kingdom as portrayed by Tulsidas.

C. Rajagopalachari in his Forword to A.G. Atkin's Ramayana wrote: "Tulsidas made his vision of God into a concrete reality for the commonest of men around him. Tulsidas could have made himself as grand or obscure as any philosopher ancient or modern; for he had learning enough for it. But he was too pious to lose himself in that manner. His great love of the common folk enabled him to produce a work that has stood the test of centuries like a rock among philosophers, pandits and lonely men and women".

Vincent A. Smith, the British biographer of Akbar the Great, referred to Tulsidas as "the tallest tree in the magic garden" a medieval Hindu poetry. "His name will not be found in the Ain-i-Akbari, or in the pages of any Muslim annalist, or in the books by European authors based on the narratives of the Persian historians. Yet that Hindu was the greatest man of his age in India — greater even than Akbar himself, in as much as the conquest of the hearts and minds of millions of men and women affected by the poet was an achievement infinitely more lasting and important than any or all of the victories gained in way by the monarch".

"It is noteworthy, observed Professor Williams, "that the Rama legends have always retained their purity, and unlike those of Brahma, Krishna, Shiva and Durga, have never been mixed up with indicencies and licentiousness. In fact, the worship of Rama has never degenerated to the same extent as that of some of these other deities".

According to Winternitz's History of Indian Literature "the Ramayana has become the property of the whole Indian people, and scarcely any other poem in the entire literature of the world has influenced the thought and poetry of a great nation for centuries". Says F.E. Keay: "The Ramayana of Tulsidas will always hold its place as the work of a great literary genius. The importance of its influence cannot be exaggerated".

Edwin Greaves in his sketch of Hindi literature says: "Tulsidas was a very real and loveable man, and in his works, he invariably still lives... The Ramayana is the work by which the author is immortalised. It is the Bible of the Hindi speaking Hindus. The Goswami's humble and devout spirit is united with an ability to use Hindi in a way which no other writer equalled. Tulsidas wrote not to display his learning, or to tickle the ears of pedants; he wrote for the people, and has had his reward. No poet in English has even been to the masses that Tulsidas has been to the people of India".

F.S. Growse in his introduction to his prose translation of the Manas says "...the book is in every man's hands from the court to the cottage and is read or heard and appreciated by every class of the Hindu community whether high or low, rich or poor, young or old. The purity of its moral sentiments and the absolute avoidance of the slightest approach to any pruriency of idea... render it a singularly unexceptionable text book".

And Sir George A Grierson saw Ramcharitmanasa as the basic code of conduct. Pandits may speak of the Vedas and Upanishads, and a few may even study them; others may say that their beliefs are represented by the Puranas; but, for the great majority of the people of Hindustan, learned and unlearned, the Ramayana of Tulsidas is the only standard of moral conduct[7].

REPRESENTATIVE SELECTIONS

Renderings in English of some representative passages from the works of Tulsidas alongwith the original text in the Devanagari script are given below:

Ramlala Nahchhu

A short, early work, the *Ramlala Nahchhu* describes colourful, festive scenes associated presumably with the wedding of Ram.

गोद लिए कौसल्या बैठी रामहि वर हो।
सोभित दूलह राम सीस पर आँचर हो।।
बतिया सुघर मलिनियां सुन्दर गावहि हो।
कनक रतन मनि मौर लिए मुसुकातहि हो।।

"Queen Kaushalya sits with Ram in her lap, the ends of her sari spreading fascinatingly over the head of the bridegroom. The comely flower-girl standing close by holds up the golden wedding headgear, studded with precious stones, and sings and smiles charmingly all the while".

Vairagya Sandipani

In the *Vairagya Sandipani* the poet's main interest is in questions of moral discipline and philosophy.

रैनि को भूषन इंदु है, दिवस को भूषन भानु।
दास को भूषन भक्ति है, भक्ति को भूषन ज्ञानु।।
ग्यान को भूषन ध्यान है, ध्यान को भूषन त्याग।
त्याग को भूषन शांतिपद, तुलसी अमल अदाग।।

"The ornament of the night is the moon, that of the day the sun. The ornament of the devotee is devotion, that of devotion knowledge. The ornament of knowledge is meditation, that of meditation renunciation. The ornament of renunciation, says Tulsi, is pure, unalloyed peace".

Janaki Mangal

In the *Janaki Mangal* the poet describes the wedding of Ram and Janaki.

वर विराज मण्डप मंह बिस्व विमोहइ।
ऋतु वसन्त वन मध्य मदन जनु सोहइ।।
लागि झरोखन झांकहिं भूपति भामिनि।
कहत बचन रद लसहिं दमक जनु दामिनि।।

"The bridegroom seated under the wedding canopy enchants the world. He shines like the god of love in the midst of a forest in spring.

"The queens cling to the windows of the palace and look out (at Ram). As they speak their teeth shine like flashes of lightning".

Ram-Charit-Manas

Woven round the central story of the *Ram-Charit-Manas*

there is a great deal of religion, mythology and philosophical exposition, which are used to formulate the poet's own devotion to Ram, who is both a personal deity and the Supreme Reality.

About the sources of his work, the poet says:

नाना पुराणनिगमागम सम्मतं यद्
रामायणे निगदितं क्वचिदन्यतोपि
स्वान्तः सुखाय तुलसी रघुनाथगाथा
भाषानिबन्धमति मंजुल मातनोति।।

"Tulsidas puts forth this captivating story of Ram obtained from various *Vedas, Puranas, Shastras* and some other sources in the language of the people for the satisfaction of his own soul".

The greatness of the theme gives him much satisfaction:

जदपि कवित रस एकउ नाहीं, राम प्रताप प्रगट एहि माही।
सोइ भरोस मोरें मन आवा, केहि न सुसंग बड़प्पनु पावा।
धूमउ तजइ सहज करुआई, अगरु प्रसंग सुगन्ध बसाई।
प्रिय लागिहि अति सबहि मम भनिति राम जसे संग।
दारु विचारु कि करइ कोउ बंदिअ मलय प्रसंग।।

"Although my work may lack poetical qualities, the knowledge that it sets forth the glories of Ram reassures me, for who will not attain greatness by good associations? Even smoke, bitter by nature, ceases to be disagreeable as soon as it is joined by the sweet smell of license. The Malaya sandalwood will continue to be worshipped because of its association with the Malaya mountain and the fact that it is only a piece of wood will not weigh will anyone".

He seeks the goodwill of all:

जड़ चेतन जग जीव जत सकल राममय जानि।
बंदऊं सब के पद कमल सदा जोरि जुग पानि।
देव दनुज नर नाग खग प्रेत पितर गन्धर्ब।
बंदऊं किन्नर रजिनिचर कृपा करहु अब सर्ब।

आकर चारि लाख चौरासी, जाति जीव जल थल नभ वासी।
सीयराममय सब जग जानी, करऊं प्रनाम जोरि जुग पानी।।

Knowing that Ram dwells in all things and beings, animate and inanimate, I bow at the lotus-feet of all, with folden hands. Be kind to me, all ye hosts of deities and demons, men, serpents, birds, ghosts ancestors, choristers of heaven, dark demons of the night. There are eighty-four lakh types of being cast in four forms which inhabit water, earth and air. Knowing Sita-Ram to be immanent, dwelling everywhere and in all, I salute all with folded folded hands".

The descriptive passages in the *Manas* are some of the best. The following reveals the feelings of Sita when the princes Ram and Lakshman appear in King Janak's flower-garden:

चितवति चकित चहूं दिसि सीता, कह गए नृप किसोर मनु चीता।
जंह विलोक मृग सावक नैनी, जनु तहं वरिस कमल सित श्रेनी।
लता ओट तब सखिन्ह लखाए, स्यामल गौर किसोर सुहाए।
देखि रूप लोचन ललचाने, हरषे निज निधि पहचाने।
थके नयन रघुपति छवि देखें, पलकन्हिहूं परिहरीं निमेषें।
अधिक सनेह देह भै भोरी, सरद ससिहि लतु चितव चकोरी।
लोचन मृग रामहि उर आनी, दीन्हे पलक कपाट सयानी।

"Sita looks eagerly all round her, wondering which way the charming princes had gone. Whichever way her fawn-like eyes cast a glance, it would look as if a shower of rows of white lotus-flowers had fallen. The girl companions of Sita pointed to a spot behind the creepers where the two, dark and fair princes stood. Sita's eyes looked greedily at their fair forms. Joy filled her heart as though she had found her lost treasure. The sight of Ram's beauty made her eyes motionless and the eyelids ceased to drop down. So overpowered was she by an excess of love that she lost control over her body. It was like the *chakor* (the traditional moon-gazing bird) looking fixedly at the moon in winter. Through the gates of her eyes she took in Ram in her heart and smartly closed the doors by shutting her eyelids".

This is how those gathered at the court of King Janak see Ram before Siva's bow is broken:

जिन्ह कें रही भावना जैसी, प्रभु मूरति तिन्ह देखी तैसी।
देखहिं रूप महा रनधीरा, मनहुं बीर रस धरें सरीरा।
डरे कुटिल नृप प्रभुहिं निहारी, मनहुं भयानक मूरति भारी।
रहे असुर छल छोनिप वेषा, तिन्ह प्रभु प्रगट काल सम देखा।
पूरबासिन्ह देखे दोउ भाई, नर भूषन लोचन सुखदाई।
नारि विलोकहिं हरषि हियं निजनिज रुचि अनुरूप।
जनु सोहत सिंगार धरि मूरति परम अनूप।।
विदुषन्ह प्रभु विराटमय दीसा, बहु मुख पर पग लोचन सीसा।
जनक जाति अवलोकहिं कैसे, सजन सगे प्रिय लागहिं जैसे।
सहित विदेह बिलोकहिं रानी, सिसु सम प्रीति न जात बखानी।
जोगिन्ह परम तत्वमय भासा, सांत सुद्ध सम सहज प्रकासा।
हरि भगतन्ह देखे दोउ भ्राता, इष्टदेव इव सब सुख दाता।

"Each saw the image of Ram according to his own mental attitude. To the warriors he was the very embodiment of valour. To crafty kings trembled to look at his mighty figure, the very image of Fear. The demons sitting in disguise felt as if Doom was staring at them. The citizens saw in the two brothers the jewels of humanity, and the delight of their eyes. To the hearts of the delighted ladies, they were rare personfications of Love and Beauty. The learned saw in the Lord the vast cosmic form with many mouths, heads, feet, eyes and hands. To King Janak's relatives, they were like their own near and dear kith and kin. In the heart of King Janak, they aroused love like that he had for his own children. To the yogis they were the Supreme Reality, motionless, pure, equal-minded, self-expressed. In the eyes of the devotees, they were their own deities who brought all manner or bliss".

Lakshman's simple faith and deep devotion are evidenced in the following lines, as he pleads with Ram to be allowed to accompany him to the forests:

दीन्हि मोहि सिख नीक गोसाईं, लागि अगम अपनी कदराई।
नरबर धीर धरम धुर धारी, निगम नीति कहुं ते अधिकारी।
मैं सिसु प्रभु सनेंह प्रतिपाला, मंदरु मेरु कि लेहि मराला।
गुरु पितु मातु न जानउं काहू, कहऊं सुभाउ नाथ पतिआहू।
जहं लगि जगत सनेह सगाई, प्रीति प्रतीति निगम निजु गाई।

मोरें सबइ एक तुम्ह स्वामी, दीनबन्धु उर अन्तरजामी।
धरम नीति उपदेसिअ ताही, कीरति भूति सुगति प्रिय जाही।
मन क्रम बचन चरन रत होई, कृपासिंधु परिहरिअ कि सोई।

"Lord, good is the advice you give me. But the coward that I am, it is beyond my reach. Only the exceptional men of fortitude, grounded in the scriptures and high morality deserve advice of such high import. I am only an infant brought up by your love. Can a young swan lift the burden of the Mandrachal and Sumeru mountains? Lord, I am telling you my sincere feelings. I have known no other teacher, father or mother. For me all relationships and bonds of affection, love and faith which bind men in the world and are extolled in the *Vedas* have come to be centred in you, dweller in our hearts. Let religion and morality be preached to those who care for reputation, power and a good end. But, Ocean of Compassion, could you give up one whose only concern is devotion to your feet in thought, speech and action"?

Moral philosophy is mixed up with a description of natural beauty when the rains set in and Ram misses Sita:

घन घमंड नभ गरजत घोरा, प्रिया हीन डरपत मन मोरा।
दामिनि दमक रह न घन माहीं, खलकै प्रीति जथा थिर नाहीं।
बरषहिं जलद भूमि निअराएं, जथा नवहिं बुध विद्या पाएं।
बूंद अघात सहहिं गिरि कैसे, खल के बचन संत सह जैसे।
भूमि परत भा ढाबर पानी, जनु जीवहि माया लपटानी।
सरिता जल जलनिधि महुं जाई, होइ अचल जिमि जिव हरि पाई।

"As the clouds gather up and burst in thunderclaps in the sky, my heart is shocked because my beloved Sita is not with me. There are flashes of lightning in the clouds, even as there is no constancy in the friendship of the wicked. The clouds come down on the plains to pour rains, even as the wise bend down with humility when they acquire knowledge. The mountains suffer the blows of the rain drops, just as the saintly suffer the speech of the wicked. Water becomes dirty as soon as it touches the earth, even as the individual soul is spoilt when it is enveloped in illusion. The waters of the river are stilled on entering the sea, even as the self is at rest in union with God".

Ram gives this assurance to Vibhishan, from the enemy camp, once he seeks refuge with him:

जौ नर होइ चराचर द्रोही, आवै समय सरन तकि मोही।
तजि मद मोह कपट छल नाना, करऊं सद्य तेहि साधु समाना।
जननी जनक बन्धु सुत दारा, तनु धनु भवन सुहृद परिवारा।
सब कै ममता ताग बटोरी, मम पद मनहिं बांध बरि डोरी।
समदरसी इच्छा कछु नाहीं, हरष सोक भय नहिं मन माहीं।
अस सज्जन मम उर वस कैसें, लोभी हृदयं बसइ धनु जैसे।
तुम्ह सारिखे सन्त प्रिय मोरें, धरऊं देह नहिं आन निहोरें।

"A person may be enemy of all the world and its animate and inanimate beings but the moment he surrenders himself to me having given up pride, illusion, hypocrisy and deceit, I transform him into one like the, noblest of men. He who gathers together the threads of his affection for his mother, father, brother, wife, body, riches, home, friend and family and waves them into a string tied to me, he who is equal minded, desireless, unmoved by joy, grief and fear—such a good man lives in my heart like riches and property in the hearts of the greedy. Saintly men are dearest to me. For them do I take this human form and for no other reason".

Vibhishan is worried that Ram is at a disadvantage against Ravan sitting well armed in his chariot on the battle field. Ram recounts the weapons that bring true victory.

सुनहु सखा कह कृपानिधाना, जेहि जय होइ सो स्यंदन आना।
सौरज धीरज तेहि रथ चाका, सत्य सीलदृढ़ ध्वजा पताका।
बलविवेक दम परहित घोरे, छमा कृपा समता रजु जोरे।
ईस भजनु सारथी सुजाना, विरति चर्म संतोष कृपाना।
दान परसु बुधि सक्ति प्रचंडा, वर बिग्यान कठिन कोदण्डा।
अमल अचल मन त्रोन समाना, सम जम नियम सिलीमुख नाना।
कवच अभेद विप्र गुरु पूजा, एहि सम विजय उपाय न दूजा।
सखा धर्ममय अस रथ जाकें, जीतन कहं न कतहुं रिपु ताकें।

"Listen friend", says the merciful Lord, "the chariot which brings victory is different. The wheels of that chariot are bravery and fortitude. Its flags are truth and moral power. Its horses are force, judgment, self control and service of fellowmen, tied to the chariot by the ropes of charity, compassion and equalmindedness. Devotion is the skilled charioteer, selflessness, the shield, contentment, the sword, charity, the axe, intelligence, the mighty bolt, the elevated mind, the terrible bow. A heart, pure and unruffied, is the quiver, while the arrows are equality, disciplined life and self-control. The impenetrable armour is worship of the teacher and the Brahmin. There are no better weapons for securing victory. Friend, for one who sits in such a chariot, there are no more enemies to be conquered".

Dohavali

Dohavali is a collection of 573 couplets in some of which the poet makes acute observations on life and manners.

मनि मानिक महंगे किए, सहंगे तृन जल नाज।
तुलसी एते जानिए राम गरीब नेवाज।।
घर कीन्हें घर जात है घर छोड़े घर जाइ।
तुलसी घर बन बीच हीं राम प्रेम पुर छाई।।
मुखिया मुखु सो चाहिए खान पान कहुं एक।
पालइ पोषइ सकल अंग तुलसी सहित विवेक।।

"It is enough to prove Ram's compassion that gold and jewels are scarce but straw, water and cereals (essential for supporting life) are easily available.

"If we build a house here (as a man of the world), we lose our (true spiritual) home; but if we renounce our hearth and home (social responsibilities), then again our home is ruined. To my mind, the best thing to do is to reside in the city of Ram which lies midway between the home and the forest.

"The chief should be like the mouth which is one for the purposes of eating and drinking but which nevertheless thoughtfully nourishes all the members of the body.

"What does it matter whether it (the language medium) is Sanskrit or the common dialect? True love is the one thing needful. If a rug serves better, what is the use of a shawl"?

Barwai Ramayana

In *Barwai Ramayana* the story of Ram is sung in the *Barwai* metre which with its soft musical qualities is specially suited for the delineation of the finer shades of feeling.

चंपक हरवा अंग मिलि अधिक सोहाइ
जानि परै सिय हियरे जब कुभिलाई।
गरब करहु रघुनन्दन जनि मन मांह
देखहु आपनि मूरति सिय कै छांह।
विरह आगि उर ऊपर जहं अधिकाइ
ए अंखिआं दोउ बैरिनि देहि बुझाई।

"A garland of (white-yellow coloured) champak flowers looks well on the person of Sita. But it mixes so well with her complexion that it is possible to distinguish it only when the flowers have faded.

"Ram do not be too proud of your appearance. Your (dark) figure is but a shadow of Sita's (resplendent) beauty.

"As soon as the fires of separation flame up in my heart, these two eyes prove my enemies for they (the tear-drops) extinguish it instantly".

Kavitavli

The *Kavitavali* is a collection of quatrains of exquisite pictorial and musical qualities dealing with the story of Ram and the story of the poet's own life and experiences.

These lines describe Sita as she leaves the city walls of Ayodhya on her way to the forest.

पुरतें निकसीं रघुवीरवधू, धरि धीर दए मग में पग द्वै।
झलकीं भरि भाल कनीं जल की, पुट सूखि गए मधुराघर वै
फिर वूझति हैं चलनो अब केतिक पनंकुटी करिहौ कित है ?
तिय की लखि आतुरता पिय की अंखियां अति चारु चलीं जल च्वै।

"Exercising all her patience and her will-power, the bride of Raghuvir came out of the city and took two steps on the path (to the forest). Soon her forehead was covered with resplendent drops of perspiration. Her sweet lips went dry. And the next moment she was asking Ram, "How much more do we have to walk? Where are you going to set up your hut of leaves?" Tears droped from the eyes of the husband as he noticed his wife's impatience and eagerness".

As Ram and Sita are passing through the forests, the village women want to know from Sita how she is related to the young prince beside her:

सुनि सुन्दर बैन सुधारस साने सयानी हैं जानकी जानी भली
तिरछे करि नैन, दै सैन, तिन्हें समुझाइ कछू मुसुकाइ चली
तुलसी तेहि औसर सोहैं सबै अवलोकति लोचन लाहु अली
अनुराग–तड़ाग में भानु उदैं बिगसीं मनो मंजुल कंजकली।

"When Sita heard the sweet nectar-like words of the village women, she at once saw through their clever question. She gave a side-glance and an understanding wink, smiled and went forward. Looking at Sri Ram with delight in their eyes, these village women themselves looked charming. It was as if lotus buds had blossomed forth in the lake love at the touch of sunrise".

Here is a lurid picture of Lanka on fire:

लगी लागी आगि भागि भागि चले जहां तहां
धीयं को न माय, बाप पूत न सम्भारहीं
छूटे बार, बसन उधारे, धूम धुन्द अन्ध
कहें बारे बूढ़े 'बारि बारि' बार बारहीं
हय हिहिनात, भागे जात धहरात गज,
भारी भीर ठेलि पेलि रौंदि खौंदि डारहीं
नाम लै चिलात बिललात अकुलात अति
'तात तात' तौंसियत झौसियत झारहीं।

"People in fright run helter-skelter crying `Fire'. Mothers do not heed their daughters, nor fathers their sons. With dishevelled hair and clothes in disarray, the fumes of smoke choking their eyes, old men and young cry out for water. Horses neigh and break away, elephants trumpet and push at the huge crowds, crushing them down under their feet. Upset and terror-stricken, everyone calls at everyone else, 'We are being baked as in an oven by these scorching flames".

The poet looks back at his early life in some passages:

जाति के, सुजाति के, कुजाति के पेटागि बस
खाए टूक सब के, विदित बात दुनीं सो
मानस वचन कायं किए पाप सतिभांय
राम को कहाइ दासु दगाबाज पुनी सो
रामनाम को प्रभाउ, पाउ, महिमा, प्रतापू
तुलसी सो जग मनिअत महामुनी सो
अति हीं अभागो, अनुरागत न रामपद

"Urged by the pangs of hunger, you had to beg at the doors of all kinds of high and low caste people. The world knows this. You won the reputation of being a man of Ram but you have not lived up to that reputation, having indulged in all kinds of evil in thought, speech and action. But behold the power, the influence, the greatness of the name of Ram; people now hail you, Tulsi, as the great sage (Valmiki). Even though you have witnessed a miracle so great as this, you have not, the luckless fool that you are, fixed yourself firmly in the love of Ram".

He is full of repentance:

भलि भारत भूमि, भले कुल जन्मु, समाजु सरीरु भलो लहि कै
करपा तजि कै परुषा वरषा, हिम, मारुत, घाम सदा सहि कै
जो भजै भगवानु सयान सोई, तुलसी हठ चातुक ज्यों गहि कै
नतु और सबै विष वीज बए, हर हाटक कामदुहा नहि कै

"You were born in this good country, Bharat, in good family, with (all the advantages of) a fine personality and good society. In such circumstances, he alone would be wise who would give up anger and harsh speech and, braving the rigours of heavy rains, cold winter, high winds and the hot sun engage himself in the love of God with the single-minded devotion of the *Chatak* bird because all else is like harnessing the heavenly cow, Kamdhenu, to a plough of gold to raise a harvest of poison".

He looks at the world and laments trends in life and society in his own times:

किसबी किसान कुल बनिक भिखारी भाट
चाकर चपल नट चोर चार चेटकी
पेट को पढ़त गुन गढ़त चढ़त गिरि
अटत गहन गन अहन अहेटकी
ऊंचे नीचे करम धरम अधरम करि
पेट ही को पचत बेचत बेटा बेटकी
तुलसी बुझाइ एक राम घनस्याम ही तें
आगि बड़वागि तें बड़ी है आगि पेट की।

"All today work only to make a livelihood—those who are taking education or resorting to various devices or ascending mountains or roaming about in dense forests in search of game. This applies to all sections of society the manual labourer, the farmer, the trader, the beggar, the minstrel, the servant, the nimble acrobat, the thief, the envoy and the magician. They will do anything, good or evil, moral or immoral, even sell a daughter or a son to fill their bellies. Tulsi says, "The pangs of hunger are more devastating than any other fires. Only the blue cloud that is Ram can extinguish this fire".

His sincerest note is heard when he sings about himself and Ram:

जागै जोगी जंगम जती जमाती ध्यान धरैं
डरैं उर भारी लोभ मोह कोह काम के
जागे राजा राजकाज सेवक समाज साज
सोचें सुनि समाचार बड़े बैरी बाम के
जागे बुध विद्या हित पण्डित चकित चित
जागै लोभी लालच धरनि, धन, धाम के
जागै भोगी भोग हीं वियोगी रोगी सोगबस
सोवै सुख तुलसी भरोसे एक रामके।

"Yogis, roving holy men, sadhus and their parties are kept

awake because they are keen to go into meditation or anxious to avoid lust, anger, illusion and greed. Kings are kept awake on account of state affairs. Their attendants and paraphernalia, the worries due to news about enemy activity. The learned keep awake in pursuit of learning; the greedy in pursuit of land, wealth and houses; the pleasure-seeker is kept awake in search of pleasure; the love-lorn and the diseased on account of the pangs of separation or ill-health. It is only Tulsi who sleeps well because of his abounding faith in Ram".

Vinaya Patrika

The *Vinaya Patrika* is a collection of devotional songs recording the poet's intimate spiritual longings and written in his most mature style. Renderings of a few songs are given below:

तू दयालु दीन हों तू दानि हौं भिखारी
हौं प्रसिद्ध पातकी तू पाप पुंज हारी।।
नाथ तू अनाथ को अनाथ कौन मोसों?
मो समान आरत नहिं आरतिहर तोसों।।
ब्रह्म तू हौं जीव तू ठाकुर हौं चेरो
तात मात सखा गुरू तू सब विधि हितु मेरो
तोहिं मोहिं नाते अनेक मानियै जो भावै
ज्यों ज्यों तुलसी कृपालु चरन सरन पावै।।

"Lord, you are full of compassion and I am indigent you are the alms-giver and I am the alms-man, I am a well-known sinner and you are the destroyer of sin. You are the lord and master of all who have none to protect them, and where is the orphan like me? There is none more miserable than I am and none who takes away men's miseries as you do. You are the Supreme Reality and I am the individual soul; you are the master, I am the servant. You are my father, mother, friend and guru, a well-wisher at all points. Many are the bonds of relationship between you and me. You may treat me as you choose. All that Tulsi asks for is that you will redeem him in the manner it is possible".

यह विनती रघुवीर गुसाई
और आस विस्वास भरोसो हरौ जीव जड़ताई।।
चहौं न सुगति सुमति संपति कछु रिधि सिधि विपुल बड़ाई
हेतुरहित अनुराग रामपद बढ़ै अनुदित अधिकाई।।
कुटिल करम लै जाइ मोहि जंह जंह अपनी बरिआई
तहं तहं जनि छिन छोइ छांड़िए कमठअंड की नाई।।
या जग में जहं लगि या तनु की प्रीति प्रतीति सगाई
ते सव तुलसीदास प्रभु ही सों होहिं सिमिटि इक ठाई।।

"This is my prayer, Raghuvir, my master. Take away all the hope, faith and trust I put in others and all the ignorance of the individual soul. I ask not for salvation or knowledge or wealth, spiritual accomplishments or surpassing greatness. All I want is that a disinterested love for your lotus-feet should grow and develop in me as the days pass by. Whatever the places to which I am driven by the force of ruthless *karma* (action entailing consequences), all I ask for is that you will not withdraw your affection for me even for a moment even as the tortoise does not part from its eggs. All love, all affection, all relationships, whatever binds this mortal frame to this world may be gathered up at a single point and directed only towards my lord and master. This is the prayer of Tulsidas".

असि कछु समुझि परत रघुराया
बिनु तब कृपा दयालु दास हित मोह न छूटै माया।।
वाक्य ग्यान अत्यन्त निपुन भवपार न पावै कोई
निसि गृह मध्य दीप की वातन्ह तक निवृत नहिं होई।।
जैसे कोई इक दीन दुखित अति असन हीन दुख पावै
चित्र कल्पतरु कामधेनु गृह लिखे न बिपति नसावै।।
षटरस बहु प्रकार भोजन कोउ दिन अरु रैनि बखानै
बिनु बोले संतोषजनित सुख खाई सोइ पै जानै।।
जब लगि नहिं निज हृदि प्रकास अरु बिषय आस मन माहीं
तुलसीदास तब लगि जगजोनि भ्रमत सपनेहुं सुख नाहीं।।

"Raghuvir, Gracious Lord and Master of the devotee, it strikes me that unreality and illusion cannot be dispelled except by your grace. No one skilled only, in verbal knowledge can get over and cross this objective world. Darkness cannot be got over by a man who is shut up in a dark chamber by night and merely talks about light and a lamp. The privation of the poor wretch who starves for want of food and nourishment will not be removed by drawing a picture of *Kalpataru* (the wish-fulfilling tree) or the Kamdhenu (the celestial cow of plenty) on the walls. The satisfaction of good meal is known only to him who eats it, even if he should not say a word; but mere talk, day and night, about the six varieties of eatables will do him no good. Tulsidas says as long as there is no illumination of the heart (no direct apprehension of reality) and the objective world of desire continues to have its hold on the mind, there is no true happiness to be had even in a dream and the individual soul goes on roaming through endless earthly incarnations".

अब लौं नसानी अब न नसैहौं।
राम कृपा भव निसा सिरानी जागे पुनि न डसैहौं।।
पायो नाम चारु चिंतामनि उर करतें न खसैहौं
स्यामरुप सुचि रुचिर कसौटी चित कंचनहिं खसैहौं।।
परबस जानि हंस्यो इन इन्द्रिन, निजक्स है न हंसैहौं
मन मघुकर पन कै तुलसी रघुपति पद कमल बसैहौं।।

"My life has been wasted upto this time. I shall allow it to go to waste no longer. By the grace of Ram, the night that is this world has come to an end. Fully awake, I shall not go to sleep again. Having found the beautiful jewel of the name of Ram, I shall not allow it to slip out of the grip of my heart. I shall put the gold of my heart to the dark-coloured touchstone of the pure and engrossing form of the Lord. As long as my faculties were controlled by others I was their laughing-stock; now that they are under my own control, I shall no more be an object of ridicule. I now that henceforth my heart like the bee shall for ever remain fixed to the lotus feet of Ram"[8].

In Search of God

Apart from the *Ramcharitmanasa* which is in itself a masterpeice, Tulsi wrote many *dohas* expressing devotion to God:

Why waste your time in searching
For God in many parts?
Just sit down and meditate—
He dwells within your hearts.

The day is lit up by the sun;
The night by the moon in its motion.
So devotion enriches each human being
And knowledge enriches devotion.
The one who loves God truly
Soars on devotion's wings;
Name or fame don't touch him
Or pain or such like things

But there are many obstacles to devotion. The first and major obstacle is pride:

Don't be proud and scorn
A poor man's poverty.
If you drop a stone in slush,
You get splashed in the eye.

It is childlike humility which really enables one to meet God:

All are very willing
To rule or lead or guide;
But he who is like a humble child
Has God by his side.

Another major obstacle to devotion is wealth, as it so easily leads to sin. Tulsi understands this well:

Wealth is dangerous;
It leads one to sin.
And when it's lost, the fire
Of guilt will burn within.

In any case wealth does not bring real satisfaction:

The worldly-wise love money;
For them wealth is a must
But if you find contentment—
All the rest is dust.

But God is not only in his heaven or in your heart. He is also in others. Unless you love and serve others you cannot even meet God or pray properly:

Treat all people well.
Perhaps, to your surprise,
The one whom you are meeting
Is God in some disguise.

Tulsi is very practical about this:

Kindness is the basic virtue;
The root of sin is pride,
Be kind; then friend, when danger comes
You'll have somewhere to hide.

An important aspect of one's relationship to others on which depends one's relationship to God is forgiveness:

An angry man will soon meet death,
Lust leads but to sin.
If I forgive with loving kindness
I find my God within.

But however much we strive towards God, we must face the fact that all of us sin and sin frequently. Tulsi, of course, is fully aware of this and deals with it practically:

Don't expect mangoes
From a thorny tree!
If you want happiness
From sin strive to be free!

As day displaces night
And night blots out the day
All holy God and sin
Cannot in one mind stay.

Sin does not only separate us from God, but also from other human beings:

The lustful and the greedy man
Who hates and insults others,
Has Satan for his guest—
No humans are his brothers.

How to get rid of sin? Tulsi knows only one answer and puts it superbly:

As salty sea-water evaporates
And comes down clean, pure rain,
So a sinner, meeting the Lord,
Is cleansed from every stain.

He makes the dumb man talk
The lame man climb the hill;
So despite my sinfulness
He will love me still.

Tulsi loved people and knew them well. He could communicate to them in their language. He knew their weaknesses and strengths. Much of his teaching is practical advice to help the ordinary person deal with every day problems:

If you treat wealth like stones
And honour girls as mothers
You will meet God—your real joy—
I guarantee, my brothers.

Your body is a field—
Virtue and vice the seeds.
O farmer, you will reap
According to your deeds.

Act in haste;
Repent at leisure,
Think ahead—
And find real pleasure.

When born you cried, while others
were filled with joy so deep;
Act so, that when you go,
You'll laugh while others weep.

Tulsi was not only a practical moralist. He was also a deep thinker. In his struggle against superstition, he seems to have attained to monotheism. This seems evident in the couplet below, even though two names are used for the deity:

I serve my God, my strength, my hope—
I live in Him alone
He may recalled by different names

For me He's only one

In all his thinking and advising, Tulsi was continually in search of God:

Before I found my God
I begged from door to door
Now He is my possession—
I am no longer poor.

But how do you meet this God?

Close the doors of your senses;
Open the door of your mind.
Then you will meet your dearest treasure—
Your God within you'll find.

The quest for God is never easy. There will be all kinds of difficulties. Tulsi illustrates through a not uncommon experience:

As the *chakora* looks at the moon,
Although his neck is strained;
So, Lord, I serve you through my life,
However much I am pained.

Ultimately in and through the world, in and through the people he serves, Tulsi comes back to his Lord—his soul's delight, his only real reward:

O Lord, in love I come
Unto your lotus feet;
I care not where I live
Or what I have to eat.
I need but you, O Lord;
You are my lover true.
My mind and heart are restless
Until they rest in you.
Men may praise or blame me—
I do not fear them, Lord.
I only want you in my heart—
You are my sole reward[9].

Tulsidas is considered the greatest poet of the Indian middle ages. His *RAMCHARITMANASA* is the greatest scripture of Hindi-speaking people. On the lips of all, the epic has surpassed Valmiki's original poem in Sanskrit.

HYMNS

Cast a glance at me, O Lord!
Though I'm not a pennyworth
Unless I do turn to you
Visage of my anguished soul.

Many a time my eyes strayed
Towards the world of tinted toys
But I'd beg you pray do not
Turn your gaze away from me.

Faith hadn't yet ripened to
Make me see things clear-eyed
Nor had I approached you to
View the glory of your face.

At your feet an offering lies
Could a cry from this mirror's
Reflection approach the one
Reflected and reflector?

View yourself in me. O Lord!
Mark your compassion, your might.
And, if you don't mind, observe
In me lowliest slave of yours.

Your name is the safest born.
Safe is one who nestles there
And resides beneath its shade.
Tulsidas is only yours
O merciful Master! you
Treat him only as you please.

O Lord! who else but you would
Listen to my woeful cry?
Unusual is my appeal:
Though a good-for-nothing tramp
I would like to be a king.
Who would favour of such talk?

Ever since the primal dawn
I've borne the pangs of hell,
I've passed through sordid births.
But I do not covet wealth
Nor I wish to liberation.
Though I know you'd bestow these.
What I long for is to serve
As a plaything for you or

Just a pebble 'neath your feet.
If You grant Tulsi this boon
He will even be your slave.
I don't mind how low I am
Born in the order of cosmos.
Whether as living being or
Inanimate, matters not.

I've heard that my Lord is
Liberator of delinquents.
I'm a seasoned miscreant
And He is my Saviour.
How pleasing is this kingship!
As mentioned in Shastras. He
Did reclaim the wrongdoers—
Ganika, Ajamil and Gajendra.
Many a sinner, by His grace.
Has accomplished salvation
E'en if unconsciously you
Chant the Name of God, you get
Sent from hell to paradise.
Knowing marvel of your Name
I fall at your lotus feet
O my Lord! says Tulsidas.

Friend, your soul won't find rest
Even in your wildest dreams
Till you have abandoned your
Lust and quest for useless things.

Devotees can't claim the Lord
Till their aims are harmonised
Through a living faith in Him

And their blazing souls are merged
Into a single flame, with love.
For only unsullied faith
Can consume trickery and fake.
You can't find a nook to sit
On the royal seat of Rama
As long as you can't address
Him with confidence and faith.
If trust and reliance merge
You get bliss at Rama's feet
And burn in the flame of love.

DOHAS

Reputation, wealth and verse
Are effective only if
Like the river of heaven, they
Lead to happiness of all

Wilder than the jungle flames
Is the stomach's fire indeed.

Carnal, diehard, rash and dim
Beggar, infamous, senile,
Lewd, immoral, misanthrope
All these are live cadavers.

Compassion is root of faith
And the source of sin is pride
Don't abandon compassion
Tulsi, as long as you breathe.

Warmly do rich folk
Greet each other but
No one bothers for
Poor Tulsidas.

Lo! My soul is bathed in light
Though there's no oil, no wick.
How to laud the wonderous ways
Of that great illuminer.

Great is power of Lord's name
Sung in sleep or while you yawn

It checks big sins like murder
Of a pandit or hundred cows.

Oration can help no one
Cross the ocean of the world
As naming a lamp at night
Can't make darkness disappear.

Fond of other's wives, sly,
Wrapped in hatred, greed and lust
Such are our seers and saints
That's mystique of iron age.

Thanks to love for saints' feet
Many a lowly man was freed
And blue blooded ones galore
Had a fall because of pride.

(*Courtsey*–Rajender Singh Verma, Singer Saints of India)

Notes and References

Ramcharitmanasa and Intellectual of Kashi

1. Shri Ramcharitmanasa.
2. Mula Gosain Charit Baba Beni Madhav Das, Grierson, Priyadas Commentary of Bhakat Mal of Nabhadas and Handoo—Chandra Kumari—Tulsidas.
3. Mancalif — History of the Sikhs.
4. Love of God and Social Duty in the Ramcharitmanas — Edmour J. Babinean. Motilal Banarsidass, Delhi 1979.
5. Tulsidas a Poet, Saint and Philosopher of the 16th century Chandra Kumari Handoo, Orient Longman, Bombay 1964.
6. Mancalif — History of the Sikhs.
7. Tulsidas — Madan Gopal — An article — Ramayan, Mahabharata and Bhagavata writers. General Editor V. Raghvan, Publication Division 1978.
8. Macalif—History of the Sikhs.
9. Saints and Sages of India — R.H. Lesser.
10. Singer Saints of India — Rajinder Singh Verma.

4

Contemporaries of Tulsidasji

There is a distinct note of relief in the opening lines of the fourth canto of the Manas, where he says that Kashi is "the homeland of Shiva and Parvati, a storehouse of knowledge and learning, a place which destroys sin and gives freedom from bondage" and that ther is no reason why he should not spend his days there.

Tulsidas's reputation as a devotee who had seen Shri Ram face to face at Chitrakut seems to have travelled and reached the people of Kashi before him. Naturally when the Ramcharitmanasa was completed and came to the notice of people, it received instant and wide recognition on account of the author's love of Ram, his absorption in the theme, the freshness of his approach, his deep humanity and the music and the movement of his following verses. It also aroused controversy because a work of the deepest import and obvious merit was written not in Sanskrit, the sacred language, but in the language of the people, because it attempted a synthesis of conflicting schools of thought and belief and, above all, because of its emphasis on a simple and direct faith, free from complicated ritual and set observances.

Society in Kashi of the Mughal times was divided into many sections. There was the circle of learned scholars versed in Sanskrit lore ; there were the members of the aristocracy; there were the leaders of various religions sects and their adherents who made a living as priests; and there were the poor, simple folk who were the victims of economic distress and social restraints. Genuine scholars like Madhusudan Saraswati recognised the merit of Tulsidas and paid handsome tributes to his skill as a poet and devotee. A few like the landed proprietor, Todarmal and possibly the linguist and pattern of letters Abdur Rahim Khan-i-Khana were drawn towards him as much by the beauty and the truth of his writings as by the purity and saintliness of his character. The people at large could not but have received his message of love, hope and faith with alarcity. But the custodians of religious sectarianism, specially the Saives, definitely disliked him because they supposed wrongly that he was trying to spread the cult of Ram at the expense of the cult of Shiva. In any case, they could see clearly that if the spirit of broadminded tolerance which he sought to promote was allowed to grow, they might soon find their occupation gone. Interested parties hatched plots to harm and humiliate him. Time honoured tradition has it that thieves were hired to steal the manuscript of the Ramcharitmanasa. The merits of the book were assailed and some of his more determined critics said that they would have nothing to do with the book unless God Shiva himself put the seal of his approval on it. The traditional lives of Tulsidas are full of stories of miracles which saved him from the attentions of his opponents. The poet makes no direct reference to their misdeeds but there are many significant passages in his works which throw light on the nature of the opposition he had to face.

Tulsidas had a deep and sincere regard for God Shiva. He had come to Kashi in the hope that God Shiva would protect him and his interests as the guardian god of the city. He fernently believed that god Shiva was both a god and a guru to him because he had derived the inspiration for the love of Ram from and through him. He had made Ram himself say, "He who opposes Shankar opposes me". But the sectarian bigots had no use for the sincerity and the nicety of the poet's position.

Tulsidas, on his part could not have liked some of the ways of "the flock of ghost worshippers" who professed allegiance to god Shiva. He disapproved of the methods of the controversialists who "back the texts of the Vedas, the Upanishads, the

Puranas and grammar like a block of wood" and "raise controversies to burn their own hearts and the hearts of others". He roundly condemned the unlettered sectarian sadhus who talked about "illusion and unreality" without really knowing anything about what they were talking about.

It is not difficult to see that this attitude of his was not in step with the times or the prevaling tendencies. Slowly but surely a regular storm of opposition gathered round him. And this opposition was not confined to wordy warfare. His opponents could go to any lengths in making him uncomfortable. In despair he tells Shiva the presiding deity of Kashi, "During the day I am jostled about by cheats and by night I am surrounded by thieves, unless you keep a kindly eye on me, my stay in this city would be made impossible".

One of the ways in which his opponents taritted him was to question his antecedents and in particular his caste, sect and upbringing. In the spirit of one almost at bay, the poet tells them in a number of passages that he had no caste and no sect and no desire to have one, that they were free to give him any names, that Shri Ram was his only Lord and master and "his enemies would meet the fate of the enemies of Shri Ram."

There are indications that attempts were made to bring about his death. He makes no direct reference to actual acts beyond saying that, with Shri Ram on his side, no one could kill him. He preferred to bear down opposition by patient sufferings. Instead of blaming others, he would sooner search his own soul and seek an explanation of his situation in his own imperfections.

There are numerous references to Kali, the Devil (representing the age of decay and evil) in his writings at Kashi. In the combat with the flesh and the Devil perhaps he had not been "sufficiently vigilant" or fully well-armed. It is a measure of his clear sightedness that he saw in the midst of all the bigotry and ill-will round him that the answer to bigotry was not more bigotry and that what really moved his opponents to action was not religion but the lack of it. If therefore, the voice of criticism died out in course of time and his opponents failed in their purposes; it was due as much to the purity of his motives and his ability to rise above the storm of passion and prejudice as to miracle and divine aid.

The favourite resorts of Tulsidas in Kashi were on the bank of the Ganga. He loved to be near the sacred river. "Drinking the water of the Bhagirathi and repeating the name of Shri Ram is my daily routine" says Tulsidas in the Kavitavali. A few spots in Kashi are specially associated with his life. He used to be the guest of his good friend Pandit Ganga Ram Joshi at Prahlad Ghat. In a chamber at Gopal Mandir he is said to have written parts of his great devotional work, the Vinaya Patrika. The god Hanuman was the poet's favourite deity and of the twelve temples of the God that he got built, one is situated at Sankat Mochan. At Assi again there is a chamber where the poet is said to have spent some of the last days of his long life.

It is certain that Tulsidas acquired a high reputation both as a poet and as a man of God in his life time. Not only poets and saints but also the people at large for whom he wrote in the language they understood flocked to him in steadily growing numbers. Two activities in which he seems to have been keenly interested were the construction of temples of Mahavir and the annual Ram Lila celebrations. At Assi Ghat he organised Ram Lila celebrations according to the story in the Ramayana and the place of south of Assi, which used to be the Lanka of these celebrations, continues to be known by that name.

One of his best friends at Kashi Pandit Ganga Ram Joshi, seems to have helped him in getting a number of temples of the god Hanuman built out of funds supplied by him. The story goes that the son of the Raja of Rajghat in Kashi lost his way while out hunting. The worried father summoned Pandit Ganga Ram Joshi to ask if the young Prince would return home. Pandit Ganga Ram Joshi promised to give an answer the following day and on return home talked to Tulsidas about the situation in which he was placed. Tulsidas, who had a lively interest in astrology, made calculations and predicted that the boy would be back home the following evening. The prediction proved true and the Raja rewarded the poet's friend by giving him a lakh of rupees which the grateful Pandit put at the feet of the poet. Tulsidas refused to touch the money but when his friend insisted he agreed to accept twelve thousand rupees which he promptly spent on the construction of twelve temples of the god Hanuman, of which the one at Sankat Mochan continues to be one of the most popular in the city.

Another good friend was Todarmal, a landowner and devoted admirer, who enjoyed the poet's confidence. It is said that the poet put a manuscript copy of the Ramcharitmanasa with him for safe custody and that it was at his instance that he was persuaded to stay on at Kashi when he had made up his mind to quit it, when Todarmal died, a panchnama (deed of arbitration) dated September 27, 1612 was drawn up under which Todarmals landed property was partitioned among his successors. A few lines at the top of this deed are said to be in the poet's own handwriting. This deed remained with the members of the family of Todarmal for eleven generations and is now in the safe custody of the Raja of Kashi. Tulsidas seldom wrote anything about human personalities, but the moving lines he wrote on the death of Todarmal reflects the depth of his feeling for the friend he had lost". The lamp of the life of a man truly large hearted, ruler of four villages, has gone out in these evil days. Once had taken upon his shoulders the burden of the love of Ram, he refused to shake it off, although there were many who asked him to do so. Now that he has gone to the world of Shri Ram, Tulsi is no longer worried, his only regret is that he will have to go through life without a pure-hearted friend". It is said that when Tulsidas had to leave Gopal Mandir on account of the opposition of the Gosains of Vallabh group, Todarmal asked him to come and stay in his own temple at Assi.

There are many stories which describe in graphis detail how the great poets and saints of the age, Surdas, Nand Das, Banarsi Das, Keshavdas, Hitharivansha, Mirabai, Abdur Rahim Khan-i-Khana, Rahim and Raskhan came in contact with Tulsidas or were moved by his poetry. In the absence of fixed dates and references in historical records, it is not possible to give credence to all of them. Nabha Das, the author of Bhaktmal and a contemporary of the poet, referred to him as an incarnation of Valmiki, "born to redeem the deprived people of his day. There are good grounds to believe that there was a great deal of mutual admiration between Tulsidas and some of these poets. It is remarkable that these poets and admirers were drawn from quarters which normally would have very little to do with one another. Followers of the Krishna Cult like Nabha Das and Nand Das who seem originally to have come to scoff remained to bless. Tulsidas was so evidently an admirer of the songs of Ṡurdas that he emulated some of them had wrote a book of songs in praise of Shri Krishna, entitled Gitavali. Banarsi Das was a Jain poet of Jaunpur, but when he wrote a poem in praise of the Ramayana, Tulsidas promptly wrote one in praise of Parshwanath in the most devout strains. The Sanskrit scholar Madhusudan Saraswati belonged to the Saiva cult but this did not stand in the way of his acknowledging Tulsidas's devotion and poetical skill after due debate. Abdur-Rahim Khan-i-Khana was a Muslim poet and administrator but the two poets had no hesitation in admiring each other. All this points as much to the esteem in which he was held as to the catholicity of his outlook[1].

In his book entitled Mul Gosain Charit Baba Beni Madhav Das had also mentioned certain names of most eminent writers, poets of that period. Shri Hitharivansha; a resident of Brindaban sent his three books entitled;

(i) Jamunastaka

(ii) Radha Sudhanidhi and

(iii) Radhika Tantra

to Goswami Tulsidasji through his disciple Navaldasa as a present. To learn Rama Raksastotra from Tulsidas swami Nandalala came from a place named Sandila. It is stated that he spent more than six months in his Company. When he was supposed to leave that place he prayed Tulsidasji to give something to him as a moment. Tulsidas gave him a Salagrama (a stone emblem of Lord Vishnu) a Kavacha (an amulet) and a blanket. There is a long list of prominent visitor or contemporaries of Tulsi, but a few most important have been mentioned below :-

Among the other dignatories who called on Tulsidas were:-

Ananya Madhava

Chitsukhacharya

Karunesa

Sadananda

Tapasvi Surari Paramhans

Virahi Bhagvanta

and Swami Vibhavananda, Dinesa and Swami Pillay from Southern parts of India. They were all fully satisfied while listening discourses of Tulsi. They were proud and feel obliged and honoured after meeting such a great saint on earth. Tulsidas was his top of glory. People come for his blessings and darshan in such a great number that it had become difficult to manage. Once he retired to his cave he refused to come out. On the persistant demands of the surging crowd one sadhu namely Dariyanand used to persuade him to come out for giving 'darshan' to the people waiting outside his cave. When it became difficult and impossible for Tulsidasji to come out of his cave time and again it was suggested to construct a high platform for Tulsidasji. Tulsi agreed to this proposal and accepted that seat constructed on a high level platform where he could remain alone and within the sight of his devotees who comes from far and wide to have a glimpse of this saint who met Shri Ram face to face at Chitrakut.

Tulsidasji spent near about eight years in Chitrakut in this manner. He felt suffocated and tired among the huge gatherings of crowds and decided to shift to some lonely place. He shifted to a nearby hill called Kamadagiri. Baba Beni Madhav Das in Mula Gosain charit has mentioned that during the year A.D. 1559 Surdasa visited him. Surdasa also showed his famous book, entitled 'Sursagar' to Tulsi. He also requested Tulsidasji for his blessing so that his beloved Lord Krishna may be pleased with him and requested that his poetry may be read throughout the world. Tulsidas picked up the book, pressed it to his heart and replied, "Lord Krishna is ever tasting the sweetness of your book, for he always fulfils the desires of His devotees. The two saints spent seven days together, afterwards Surdas returned to Brindaban[2].

In memory of his meeting with Tulsidas, Surdas wrote the following poem in praise of Tulsi.

Blessed am I to have come to the lotus feet of the best amongst the holy ones.

Having rested my eyes on his joyful face I am filled with happiness.

Casting his compassionate glance on me, he has taught me the essence of truth,

And has destroyed the root of my doubts and diffusion regarding work, worship and knowledge.

He has sung the lila of God, hearing which the hairs of my body stand on end and my mind is at peace.

Speaking words sweet as nectar while contemplating on Sita and Ram, he has satisfied me.

By meeting the holy Tulsi, flawless, wondrous and of unparalleled purity,

Surdasa has attained the goal of life by the vision of the dual divine forms[3].

In a reply to a letter of Mirabai through a song included in Vinaya Patrika Tulsidas spoke thus:

Those who do not love Sita and Rama,
Though they be your dear ones,
Give them up like a million enemies.
Prahlada gave up father and Vibhishana his brother,
Bharata disowned his mother and Bali his guru,
The gopis disregarded their husbands,
But the result was joyful and good
Love and serve only those
Who accept relationship to Rama
What is the use of collyrium
If it destroys the eyes?
What more can I say?
Only they are worthy of respect
And are dearer than life,
Who help in attaining
Devotion to Rama's feet;

And this is my opinion
Says Tulsidas[4]

Notes and References

Contemporaries of Tulsidasji

1. Macaulif — *History of the Sikhs*.
2. *Mula Gosain Charit,* Baba Beni Madhav Dass.
3. Tulsidas, Chandra Kumari Handoo / This Poem was published in the Kalyan's special issue "Manas special Number, 1938, p. 2.
4. *Vinaya Patrika* and quoted by *Chandra Kumari Handoo* in her book Tulsidas, pp. 35-36.

5

Miracles of Tulsidas

Goswami Tulsidasji's life is full of miracles as recorded by Baba Beni Madhav Das. Different authors/scholars have related these miracles in their own styles. We have selected a few of them for the general knowledge and interest of our readers.

There was a merchant by the name of Jaitpal. He suddenly passed into a state of peace. His dutiful wife, abandoning every thing that was dear to her with the Lord of her life in her heart, started to burn herself with him. In a cleared forest by the bank of the Ganga, they lighted a great funeral pyre. She arranged herself for the occasion in the spirit of one already possessing a husband, and walked gaily along. Just when she walked by the cave of Tulsidas. She came alone in order to make him a namaskar. Tulsidas was repeating the names of Shri Ram his beloved God. She bowed herself prostrate on the ground. He gave her this blessing May you have eight sons. The good woman said to the bhakta of Vishnu, 'My husband has reached the state of eternal sleep and I am on the way to accompany him, abandoning all that is dear and my own. You have given me this blessing that I should become the fortunate mother of eight sons and be endowned with a husband. That word of yours will prove true, and yet I have my doubts'. Tulsidasji said 'I spoke without knowing your condition, but my Lord Shri Ram will make it true'. When that woman heard the blessings of saint Tulsidas, she bowed before him. When she reached near the dead body of her husband, she found her husband in a sitting posture. This unexpected miracle overjoyed every one present there. The woman concerned took her husband by his hand, and took him to the hermitage of Goswami Tulsidasji. There she alongwith her husband paid loving obeisance. All the inhabitants of Banaras sang the praise of Tulsidas. They exclaimed, 'Blessed is this Vaishanav. He is a complete Saviour for us dull-minded persons. Once he caused the stone bull to eat food, and by his word of blessing brought a corpse to life'. Then some one went and conveyed this news to the king.

When this incident occured in Banaras the king of India, Akbar the great was at Delhi where somebody informed him. He then made an attempt to see the miracle. He called his wise ministers and informed them of his thoughts. He said, I want you to bring about a meeting with the Vaishanava Tulsidas. I wish you to send a messanger, who is exceedingly learned in the knowledge of Brahma who is a remarkably clever speaker, and who will incline Tulsidas's mind to come here. Take a palanquin and carriage and bring him here as early as possible. I wish to see for myself what I have heard by the ear. The minister said to him, 'Your command is my authority'. He took some wise and clever speakers alongwith some of his army and reached Banaras. Coming to the hermitage of Tulsidas they stayed there that day. The news was conveyed to him that the king had called him. They said, 'The king has heard of you, as a most extraordinary God loving Vaishnava bhakta. The king has sent us because of his desire to see you'. Hearing this request, Tulsidas thought to himself, I must turn all the inhabitants of that country to repeating God's name. If the noble Vaishnavas are free from selfish desire, why should they wander from country to country? Because it is truly Hari's command that they should save mankind. Evil and ignorant men are surrounded by dark ignorance. In order to save them, good men wander about. The king as we have seen has sent a messanger and every one has heard the news'. Tulsidas the God-loving bhakta at once started. Enthusiastically repeating the names of Hari, he quickly arrived at Delhi. The king came forward and fell at his feet. The king then seated Tulsidas on his throne and whispered a command to his servants, not to allow him to return. He worshipped him with the sixteen materials for worship. The king said to Tulsidas, 'I have heard of your wonderful power and that you have got yourself made into a God. You made the stone bull eat food. In the giving of a blessing, you brought a corpse to life. Your deeds seems impossible to me. I do not understand your power'. Tulsidas said to him, It is all the doing of Shri Ram. I am but a helpless person who has placed his heart at the feet of Shri Ram. Hearing this the king said to him, cause me to meet Shri Ram. If you do not do so, I shall surely not allow you to go from here. Thus speaking, the king went into his palace. He said, if he will show me a manifestation of Ram, then only will I regard Tulsidas as a noble Vaishnava. While Tulsidas sat on the throne the servants said to him, 'You are not to be allowed to go from here. Without losing a moment give the king a sight of Shri Ram. If you do not grant this, he certainly will not allow you to leave from here.

Hearing the threatening orders of the officials of the Mughal Darbar, Tulsidasji began to remember and praise Maruti (Pawan Puttar Hanuman). Hearing the prayers of Tulsidas Maruti at once appeared and met Tulsidasji. Tulsidasji said, I am in extreme distress and, therefore, I have thought of you. And now remove this distress and increase the glory of the names of God. Maruti then performed a wonderful miracle. He called together his army of monkeys and many mighty heroes started from Heaven. Just as during the rainy season clouds appear in the sky; or as when the rain falls on the earth the grass begins to sprout; or as during the time of famine a cloud of locusts appears in the sky; so suddenly this army of monkeys ten thousand in number appeared. The monkeys boured to Maruti, and said to him, 'Please tell us what your command is'. Maruti replied to them, 'I have called you together in order that you may show to the king some of your natural characteristics. As soon as they received this command, the monkeys became full of action. They climbed upon the roofs and began to destroy the tiles. The pulled up big trees by the roots, and threw them at the peoples. There was a great alarm felt in Delhi, and a great outcry. They broke the noses of some of them and cut off their ears, they twisted off the necks of some. They grabbed some by the legs and started upwards. As women were going to the river Jamuna, with water jars on their heads, they snatched their clothes from them and threw them into the river. As father-in-law and mother-in-law were passing out of the alleys, the monkeys seized them, and fastening their beards and braids of hair together, then ran away. Those who did not worship Shri Ram, or persecuted the bhaktas of Vishnu, the monkeys lifted them up and threw into the striking drains. The evil minded merchants never gave food to anyone; the monkeys broke open their store-rooms and carried away their contents. There was a great outcry in the city. Then they entered into the palace of the king and cut off noses and ears. This also made a great outcry. The five hundred wives of the king were all seated in the company of his concubies. The monkeys came threw dirty water on them. They suddenly seized all evil men who were thieves, adulterers and crooked in their lives. They lifted them up and took them from the palace and threw them down from above. They seized the garments and ornaments, and flew with them into the sky and then with great pleasure gave them to the poor or those who lacked food. They made the poor rich. They robbed the merchants. They beat those who spoke untruth. The servants of the king hastened to inform him what was taking place. They said, 'An army of monkeys has arrived, and they are destroying every thing. Just as when a cloud pours down a heavy rain, the sky is dense with clouds, so Delhi seems crowded with this army of monkeys. The monkeys showed great anger, and there were great outcry in the city. The king remarked 'The time for destruction of all things seems to have arrived'. There were some wise men present who said to the king, 'Tulsidas is a Vaishnava. You should not persecute him. If the monkeys increase in their anger, they will turn the whole city of Delhi upside down'. The king thought all this very remarkable, and confessed that he had committed a great fault. When Durvas persecuted Ambarisba, he had to be humiliated. So, it has happened to me. I am reminded of my justice. So he came to Tulsidas and there joining his hands palm to palm, he stood before him. Akbar said to him, 'O bhakta of Vishnu, restrain this army of monkeys. I persecuted you, because in my ignorance I did not know what I was doing. Duryodhan suffered humiliation when he attempted to persecute the good Draupadi. So it has happened to me by my persecuting you. Hearing this pity-arousing request, Tulsidas said to him, 'You were wishing to see Shri Ram. It is His army that has arrived. Just as when the sun arises at dawn, and its light spreads all over the world, so this great hero has come with an advance guard, O King. Hearing produces desire. Meditation produces devotion to listening and a direct manifestation of God produces in one a desire to know more of Him. So the monkeys are arriving first, and Shri Ram is following them. An army of 18 billions are following these monkeys. These eighteen billion monkey warriors will be followed by Shri Ram. Your good fortune has no limit. Shri Ram is coming to see you. Hearing this the king said, 'I have already seen enough of Shri Ram'. So saying he grasped him by his feet and said, I did not understand his power. If an army of ten thousand monkeys has wrought such destruction, then if the army of eighteen billions should come it would mean the end of the world. Hearing the king's pity-arousing request, the monkeys became invisible and all men worshipped the feet of Tulsidasji.

Tulsidas remained here for a year, and in great love he daily sang the praises of the extraordinary deeds in Shri Rama's life. All the inhabitants in Delhi began now to repeat constantly the names of God. And the ignorant and dull minded became wise through association with him.

Tulsidas now took leave of Akbar and went to see and worship Shri Krishna at Mathura. At first he came to Gokul and bathed by the bank of Jamuna river. Having seen and worshipped Shri Krishna he departed from there. From there he came to Vrindavan. There he made an obeisance to Shri Krishna. He remained there for a month and danced in the praise-services devoted to Hari. From there he came to Mathura. He bathed by the banks of the Jamuna. He saw and worshipped Shri Krishna and met there many Vaishnavas. In Mathura, Gokul and Vrindavan, live many Vaishnavas (those who worship only Vishnu as the one God). They are constantly engaged in singing the praises of Hari, and are always repeating His names day and night.

There was a Brahmin citizen named Priyadas of supreme piety, and a Vaishnav. Bhakti, knowledge and indifference to worldly things, were his characteristics[1].

Tulsidasji was staying with a devotee named Dhanidas at a village called Bela Patar. One day he told to Tulsidas, that I am a great sinner. When asked he related to Tulsidasji that in my morning prayer when I offer any kind of food to my Lord, the rats usually spoiled it, but on the contrary I propagate among the devotees that God Almighty had accepted the offering Himself. To know this news there had been a great excitement among the people. When the news spread far and wide the local Raja namely Raghunath Singh came to visit Dhanidas. He was much annoyed and angry to see his exploitation. Raja severally warned him that if the God Almighty did not eat in his presence he would lose his life. The Raja gave him one month's time to perform his miracle. Dhanidas was very badly upset as the time was going to expire the other day. Tulsidasji consoled him, and assured him his help, said, Do not worry. The next morning in the light of Tulsidasji instructions, Dhanidas prepared the required food as usual and in the presence of a large number of devotees and on lookers, the God Almighty was supposed to be seen taking offerings ! Sensing the importance of the situation, Tulsidasji prayed Shri Ram, with the request to fulfil the desire of the false devotee. When the food was presented to the Lord it was accepted by Him in the presence of Raja Raghunath Singh alongwith a big crowd. After this incident Goswami Tulsidasji was then invited and suitably honoured by the Raja and at the suggestion of Tulsidasji the name of village Bela Patar was changed as Raghunathpur by which name the village is known till date.

The devotees of Shri Rama from Ayodhya a most beautiful image of Shri Ram was being brought somewhere from Southern part of the country with the motive of installing the same in a newly built temple at Ayodhya. When they were taking rest on the banks of the river Jamuna near Brindaban, a Brahmin namely Uday Prakash galanced at the image, he was so impressed he determined in his mind not to allow these persons to carry away it from Brindaban to any other place. Fortunately Tulsidasji was visiting Brindaban that day. Uday Prakash the Brahmin approached Tulsidasji and expressed his inner desire to him, and requested for help to do the needful. When the persons concerned who were carrying the image started for their onward journey it so happened that they realised that image of Shri Rama had become too heavy to be carried further. In the meantime Tulsidas had reached there, and named the image 'Son of Kaushalya (Kaushalya Nandan) and installed there ceremonially as a living symbol of the Divine.

In one of his travels across the country Tulsidasji met a strange incident. Due to an irony of fate the daughter of a Zamindar of Charvari was married to another woman by mistake. This peculiar situation arose in the under mentioned story:- The mother of the girl bridegroom had not been blessed by the God with a son. When she gave birth to a daughter, she brought up her daughter like a boy. While the girl was still growing up whosoever suspected about her sex was being heavily bribed by the mother of the said girl. The mother of the girl foolishly kept this secret and even went to the extent of celebrating her wedding with another young girl. When the parents of the bride came to know about this deception they were furious and unable to control by anybody. In this hour of distress they approached Tulsidasji for his guidance and advice. Keeping in view their pathetic position, Tulsidas recited the Ramcharitmanasa for nine days. After which for the joy and happiness of everyone concerned the sex of the husband of the girl changed and became a man.

It is said that once a man named Bhulai Sahu of Kalvara caste, expired and his dead body was being carried to the cremation grounds. It was a well fact that during his life time he had always accused and abused Tulsidasji. His weeping wife was also following the funeral procession of her husband. On the way she happened to meet Tulsidasji, she saluted the great saint by touching his feet. Unaware of the situation Tulsidas blessed her, saying 'May you ever remain under the protection of your husband (Subhagyawati Bhav. सौभाग्यवतीभव). The woman explained that unfortunately she had already become a widow. Tulsidas sent for the dead body and put a few drops of Ganga Jal into the mouth of the dead body which came to life. Another version is that Tulsidas advised the party not to cremate the body till he comes back. He went back, took bath and prayed for about hours. Meanwhile the dead man got up as if from a sound sleep and asked why have you brought me here ?

Once a brahmin named Chandra, who had committed a murder, came to Kashi and frow a distance of Tulsidasji hermitage, called out the name of Shri Rama, Shri Ram, Shri Ram, Shri Ram thrice loudly. Pleased to listen the name of Shri Ram, Tulsidas got up at once and warmly embraced Chandra, served him with food and said great devotion:

> Tulsi will give the skin of his body to make the shoes
> of him who even accidently utters the word Rama

This news spread like wild fire in Kashi and a large number of Vedanti assembled in the hermitage of Tulsidas demanding explanation from Tulsidas who had committed a great sin by purifying a great sinner like Chandra brahmin. The learned Vedanties asked Tulsidas ! O greatest among the greats and holiest among the holly men ! how can you purify such a dreaded person who had committed such a great sin ? Tulsidasji replied to them very politely. Through the glory of the Divine name. Please go and study your Vedas, and Puranas then kindly let me know where I am wrong ? The learned Pandits replied, No doubt we have also gone through the scriptures that the name of God washes away all sins, but we failed to believe it. Tulsidasji advised them to choose the method which could remove their doubts and satisfy them. The Pandit suggested well, if Nandi on which Lord Shiva rides should accept food from sinner Chandra's hands, he would be welcomed as being purified. The experiment was tested and proved totally successful. The entire temple complex filled with acclamations of the assembled crowd and the doubts raised by a group of Vedanties was dispelled because they all have witnessed the miracle of the stone image of Nandi coming to life for a while to have food from Chandra—the sinner.[2]

Priyadas the well known commentator of Bhakatmal wrote a book in Sanskrit, describing the extraordinary deeds of bhakats of Vishnu in this Kali Yuga. Tulsidas heard that he had written this book containing the stories of saints. So on a certain occasion he came to visit Priyadas. He said, 'O Swami, you have written the stories of saints. I have not listened to them. Bring me the book and show it to me'. Priyadas replied, I have described the bhaktas belonging to the four generations. But I have not included in this book the noble deeds of Tulsidas. Even the Vaishnava bhakats of Kali Yuga were described in that book. Therefore Priyadas felt very much troubled. Just then a very wonderful thing happened. Unknown to Priyadas, Shri Ram came there and with his own hands wrote the story of Tulsidas. In order to listen to the book, all the Vaishnavas assembled and sat in the Assembly hall by the great door of the temple. Clever and wise Pandits also sat down to listen. Priyadas the God-loving bhakta read aloud from the book. All the Vaishnavas admired the book that was written by Priyadas. It was Tulsidas who said to him that it was Shri Hari who spoke through his lips. Hearing this remark made by the saint (Tulsidas), Priyadas said to them 'Shri Ram' came and wrote the whole history of Tulsidas. All the noble Vaishnavas now examined the hand writing of Shri Ram. The power of bhaktas is great. Neither Vedas nor Shastras are able to describe it. In attempting to describe the characteristics of Shri Hari the eighteen Puranas had to remain silent and the six Shastras had to acknowledge that they did not understand His power. If one constantly listens to this explanation of the book with pleasure he will certainly have a sight of Shri Ram. Thus the beloved of Shri Ram, the full avatar of Valmiki, and his story recorded by Shri Rama's own hand. Priyadas first book was in the Sanskrit language. After that Nabhaji wrote in the Gwalior language. After listening to its verses Mahipati had written this book in Marathi language, just as the milkman adds a little water to his milk. As in setting a diamond in a gold ornament, lacquer is used in the act of placing it, so, you saints and nice people have listened to my uncouth language. It is God Himself who is describing the life of Tulsidas; listen to it therefore, with reverence. Those who do so, assume the form of Shri Ram. The husband of Rukmani, Dweller by the banks of the Bhima, is the real Author of this book. Mahipatis name appears in these verses, but the real writer is Shri Ram. In listening or reading of this book the God Almighty the Lord of the world will be pleased[3].

Notes and References

Miracles of Tulsidas

1. Mahipati's stories of Indian saints from Bhaktavijaya.
2. Mula Gosain Charit Baba Beni Madhav Das, Priyadas (Bhakat Mal) Handoo — Tulsidas etc. etc.
3. Mahipatis stories of Indian Saints from Bhaktavijaya.

6

Who summoned Tulsidas, Akbar-the Great or Jahangir

There is a great confusion among the approach of various authors that some of them has record that Mughal Emperor Akbar-the Great called on or summoned Tulsidas to perform his miracles before him and many other learned authors have connected the name of Jahangir (1605-1629). I deem it fit to clarify this confusion for the interest of the readers of my book which I have written with great love, affection and devotion:-

Mahipati in his Marathi book entitled, Bhaktavijaya has narrated the following two incident though they have already been written in the previous chapters of this book. I am repeating these only to explain and apprised to my readers about the historical facts.

In his first incident Mahipati has recorded that it happened one day that king Akbar was going on a tour. Tulsidas immediately joined him and went with him. This happened after his marriage. The second incident which he has quoted in his book is that when Tulsidasji mericulously saved Jaitpal even after his death, and this news reached Akbar he was summoned to Delhi. About the first incident I do not want to make any comment as there is no mention of any period. Regarding the second one it is very clear that it is not correct as Mughal Emperor Akbar-the Great had never made Delhi as his capital. He ruled India from Agra and Fatehpur Sikri. After his demise he was burried at

Sikandra. I think due to some confusion or misunderstanding Mahipati has mentioned Akbar's name instead of Jahangir. For more details and clarifications I give below the most important events of Tulsidasji's life in a chronological order:-

Goswami Tulsidasji was born during July-August 1497 A.D. (Samvat 1554, 7th day of Sravana). His foster mother expired during January 1503, when he was only 5 years and 5 months old. His sacred thread ceremony was performed during February 1505 A.D. (Samvat 1561; on the occasion of Vasanta Panchami). He was married with Ratnavali during the month of June, 1526 A.D. (Samvat 1583, 13th day of Jetha). Babar the first Mughal Emperor died on (1526-1530). Humayun ruled India during 1530-1540. Akbar was born on 15th October 1542 and ruled India during 1556-1605. His wife Ratnavali died during the month of June - July 1532 A.D. (Samvat 1589, 11th day of Asadha). Had a vision of Shri Ram during the month of Jan. - Feb. 1549 A.D. (on the auspicious occasion of Mauni Amavasya, Samvat 1607). Had a meeting with Surdasa during the year 1559 A.D. (Samvat 1616 early period) started writing Shri Ramcharitmanasa during the month of March-April 1574 A.D. (Samvat 1631; Rama-navami). Completed Shri Ramcharitmanasa on the occasion of the wedding ceremony of Shri Rama and Sita (Samvat 1633 in the month of Margasirsa. Thus the book was written in 2 years, 7 months and 26 days. Collection of the verses of the Dohavali during 1583 A.D. (Samvat 1640). Copied Valmiki Ramayana during December 1584 (Samvat 1641). Started writing of the Satsai, Sita Navams, during the year 1585 A.D. (Samvat 1642). Death of his close friend Todarmal during the year 1612 A.D. (Samvat 1669). Visit of Mughal Emperor Jahangir in the year 1613 A.D. (Samvat 1670) and death of Tulsidasji during the year 1623 A.D. at the ripe age of 125 years 11 months and 7 days.

Some authors are of the opinion that the person named Todar Mal, who was an intimate friend of Tulsidas was non other than his namesake, the famous finance minister of Akbar the Great, but this also not seems true. One author has written that on the request of Todar Mal, Mughal Emperor Akbar agreed to award Tulsidas an official rank of a manasabadar, but

Tulsidas rejected the offer. His spirited reply was given in the following verse:

I am a servant of Raghunath
My deed of gift has been written,
In the court of the Lord
Now it is useless for Tulsi
To accept the office of a mere man
Brief's note on Akbar's life
(15th October 1542 - 17th October 1605)

Akbar was the son of the soil he ruled over for forty-nine years, eight months and three days. He was born on Sunday 15 October 1542, at Amarkot, a small town of less than five thousand inhabitants amidst the forbidding sand-hills of the eastern extremity of the Sind desert. The adjoining sea of sand in Rajputana provided a bleak backdrop for the birth of a child destined to rank among the great sovereigns of the world. This was not the first time that Providence chose a grim setting to raise the curtain for an important event in history.

Humayun and his 15 year old consort, Hamida Banu Begum, had reached Amarkot on 22 August 1542, following a perilous march from near Jodhpur through a track of desert as forbidding in its scarcities as in the hostility of its Rathor ruler, Rana Maldeo. It was indeed a wonder that the fleeing Mughal Emperor and his small band of followers escaped death or capture at the hands of one whom Muhammad Qasim Farishta described as "the most powerful and influential prince of the time in Hindustan". Ambition led Maldeo to forget the traditions of chivalry associated with the house of Rana Sangram Singh. His promises of support and asylum to Humayun were mere snares to entice him to Jodhpur and then hand him over to Sher Shah at a price. Timely warning by a Rana's courtier, who was once in the service of the Mughal at Agra, saved the fugitives from falling into the trap.

Humayun and his panic stricken entourage were then left with no alternative but to accept the invitation of Rana Virsal Prasad to make Amarkot the base for gaining foothold in Sind.

Hopelessness bred in Humayun and his men a desperation which enabled them to win the battle against hunger, thirst and the raiding parties of pitiless pursuers. Humayun and Hamida Banu entered Amarkot at the head of a weary troupe of seven attendants; the rest struggled in several hours later in small batches. The gallant Rana not only gave the royal couple a gracious welcome; he received every member of the Mughal Party with courtesy and made suitable arrangements for their stay and entertainment. For occupation by Humayun and his young wife he vacated his own palace inside the fort, and ordered his courtiers to do them homage in the manner done to their own sovereign.

When the Rana came to know that Hamida was seven months with a child, he placed at the disposal of his guests the meagre medical resources of his desert kingdom. Rajput ladies of high status were deputed to keep her company and to see that the memories of her arduous trek through the desert did not in any way disturb her equanimity. In a signed circular to his officers, the Rana wrote:

We have the privilege of playing the host to a royal Mughal couple. Fortune has not been kind to them in recent months. It is our moral obligation to make them feel at home in our realm and to leave nothing undone to restore their peace of mind. Therefore, I command you all, in the name of our traditions and canons of honour, to extend to them such courteous submissions as would bring them happiness. Akbar was born on 15 October 1542 at Amarkot.

...Humayun himself entered Delhi on 23 July 1555, thus ending a fifteen years period of exile. The fatwa was read in his name the same day. Akbar accompanied his father to the royal mosque for thanks giving prayers.

...It was in November 1555 that Akbar left Delhi, at the head of a sizable expeditionary force, to take charge of his new post. Bairam apprehended that Abul Ma'ali might rebel and try to retain by force the province for himself. His fears, however, proved unfounded.

Soon after reaching Lahore, Akbar launched a three pronged probing assault on positions known to be held by Sultan Sikander. Accompanied by Bairam Khan, he himself established a camp at Kalanaur; fifteen miles from Gurdaspur from where roads branched off in different directions. His plan was to rush reinforcements to any place where fighting against the remnants of the Afghan army might flare up. Little did he know that at this very time events were taking place in Delhi which were to force him to change his military plans.

On 24 January 1556, Humayun while descending the steep steps of his Library at a Din-Panaals (at old Fort; known as Pandavoan Ka Qila or Purana Qila), six miles from Delhi, slipped and rolled down the stairs, falling headlong on the ground. After remaining unconscious for two days, he breathed his last on 26 January 1556. For fear of uprising, the death was kept a closely guarded secret for seventeen days during which period contingents of the Mughàl army were placed at all vulnerable points.

The news of the passing away of the Emperor was sent to Akbar at Kalanaur through Shaikh Nasir Quli, a courtier of distinction and long standing. Akbar was dumbfounded at this sudden development and tended to favour immediate return to Delhi. But Bairam Khan thought otherwise. In his opinion it was unsafe to leave Punjab unguarded. Sultan Sikander was still at large. It was certain Sikander would make a desperate bid to come back once it was known that there was a power vaccum in the province. The situation was fraught with graver possibilities. One wrong step could have led to neutralization of all gains since the victory at Sirhind. In this crisis, Bairam Khan stood firm like a rock. Averse to taking chances, he decided to move step by step first to consolidate his position in the Punjab and then to turn eastwards to liquidate the centres of resistance that might spring up around Delhi and its neighbourhood.

On 14 February 1556 Akbar was crowned Emperor on an improvised wood-and-brick throne at Kalanaur. (The thrown at Kalanaur was eighteen feet long and three feet high. It is now a protected monument). The insignia of sovereignty had been sent to Akbar from Delhi by Tardi Beg Khan. The coronation ceremony of a king destined to be classed among the great monarches of the world was as devoid of pageantry as was his birth fourteen years earlier in the desert place of Amarkot. In the meantime, it was announced in Delhi that Jalal-ud-Din Muhammad Akbar had ascended the throne and that all was quiet throughout the length and breadth of the empire.

There are moments in history when time seems to run backwards. The death of Humayun was one such point in the annals of the Mughals. It was only six months earlier that he reoccupied Delhi after an exile of fifteen long years.
(*Courtsey*: Akbar by Muni Lal—Vikas Publishing House, New Delhi, 1980.)

When after Akbar, his son Jahangir took over the reign of power since 1605-1629 he must have summoned Tulsidasji to Delhi. The students of history are well aware that Jahangir's Insaf or justice was well known and called Adal-e-Jahangir.

The people of India still remembered that during his regime he got killed Sher Afghan and married with his wife Nur Jahan and on the popular protest of the masses Jahangir miserably failed to penalise the persons concerned they were got sunked in the river Ravi. This is the same Mughal king Jahangir who got killed Guru Arjun Devji mercilessly. Now it is clear that this was not the Mughal Emperor Akbar the great but Jahangir who invited Tulsidasji in Delhi or at Lahore and faced the consequences, Akbar the great was being poisoned by his son Jahangir through a Hakim named Fili who was attending Akbar during his illness.

In the History of the Sikhs Lord Maucaliff has also recorded that it is, however, difficult to substantiate or disbelieve entirely the story-about his visit to the Mughal Emperor in Delhi. It is said that Emperor Jahangir on hearing about the miracles he had performed asked the poet to be his guest and to demonstrate his powers. The official historians of the day make no mention of this and the vague hints thrown out by the poet are not enough to give us a clear picture of what really took place. Priyadas in his commentary on the Bhaktmal says that when the poet met "the Badshah of Delhi" and the latter asked him to show miracles, Tulsidas replied, "These stories about miracles are false. One should put one's faith in Shri Ram alone", which certainly is a reply in the poet's characteristic manner.

It is certain that during the later years of his life at Kashi, Tulsidas was a celebrity and some of the very important people of the day would come to see him. The poet himself does not seem to have been keen to establish contacts with the high and the mighty. Some at least of his visitors would have to go back disappointed because he was writing or lost in meditation. "There are indications that he was a little uncomfortable when he found that he was being sought after by people in high places". Time was he tells us, "when I begged from door to door, and now the rulers of the land are at my feet" and he knew the reason why. Those were the days when, 'Tulsi was without Shri Ram', and now Shri Ram as by his side. That the lord had "turned a handful of dust into one mightier than the mountains", that he was being hailed as one of "the great sages of the day" was the Lord's own miracle but Tulsidas seems to have remained unspoilt by this turn in his fortunes. "If a lean and poverty-stricken grass" cutter, he says, "should come by a mountain load of gold, this would remove only the poverty of his house, not the poverty of his heart. Having passed through both the phases of poverty and prosperity and having found both doubly distressing, Tulsi has blackened the face of poverty itself. He has ceased to be deluded by hope, having entered the service of Shri Ram, the River of Compassion". He realised that mere material advancement was not good for a man's spiritual health and was constantly reminding himself that the Lord was his only refuge.

There are many stories of the miracles which Tulsidas performed during this period of his life and these have been repeated so often and so consistently in the writings of poets and saints that it may be legitimately supposed that the simple and devout people among whom they were current did take them on their face value. It is easy to see that some of the veneration in which he was held did rest on his reputation as a miracle-worker who lived a charmed life. Quite a few of them, however, reveal his personality much more than his powers. He himself was so humble and gentle and utterly straightforward that it is difficult to associate any desire to indulge in magic or mystery with his dealings. It is more likely that the miracle that worked most powerfully on men's mind was his transparent sincerity his calm unruffled mind, his wide tolerance and his compassion for the erring and the distressed.

During the years at Kashi he received a great deal of recognition and went out on many of his travels in Uttar Pradesh and Bihar, but his main interests were writing and meditation. It was during these years that he attained new heights of creative literary work and spiritual self-realisation.

His Message

A Hallo surrounded the name of Tulsidas, the saint and author of the Ramayana but this should not prevent us from looking at the very human, lovable and friendly man behind his writings. He had his full portion of life's rebuffs and handicaps. He was a pauper in childhood, his home life was wrecked when he was a youth; he was assailed from all sides when in middle of his life he decided to settle down in Kashi. It is a measure of the man's will to succeed that after every set back he decided not to yield but to strive and pursue his quest with renewed vigour. "It is easy to talk out it but endless are the difficulties in the way with which only those who have pursued the path are familiar". But with all his high seriousness and fortitude he seems to have been a remarkable, gentle and lovable man who would never make an enemy if he could help it. "A friend of the friendly a lover of Ram, free from malice or rancour, detached, natural and simple in his dealings, he won the confidence of all who came in contact with him. Detached he certainly was in the sense that he could rise above public praise or criticism, but the impression that he was a recluse who did not encourage visitors and remained shut up in his study in very wide of the mark. He would not have been the welcome guest that he was in hall and hamlet during his long journeys to distant places, if he had shunned company. During the course of a journey to the eastern districts of Uttar Pradesh, he was hosted by Rajas and important men on the way, but when he reached a village the inhabitants of which were known to be cruel and vicious, he refused to accept their hospitality. He preferred to stay outside the village with a milkman and was so pleased with his humble host that he granted him the boon that the members of his family would remain Shri Rama's devotees, if they did not steel or make trouble for others. That a religious man like him should have been asked to witness a deed of arbitration drawn upto partition the estate of the landowner, Todarmal, shows both the confidence he enjoyed as an upright citizen and his readiness to do his duty to the memory of a dead friend.

The people who disliked him were the custodians of the vested interests of caste, creed and sect. They stopped at nothing in trying to bring about his discomfiture and hound him out of Kashi. But it is a measure of his tolerance that he bore no ill-will towards them and trusted that his God Ram would safeguard his interests. As he puts it, "Some say this Tulsi does a lot of evil, some say he is an impostoz, some others say that he is a sincere servant of Shri Ram, the saintly take me for a great saint, the villian for great villian. The waves of a million such true and false reports gather up around me. I ask no favours nor do I complain. I bear with all and do not let my heart be perturbed. The good and the evil which will befall Tulsi are in the hands of Shri Ram. Varily, I am like the grass which thrives only in the soil of the love of Shri Ram".

Tulsidas's tolerance stemmed directly from this mental outlook and was much more than a mere rule of conduct. Knowing that this whole world was pervaded by Shri Ram, he could not but salute everyone with folded hands.

Nevertheless, a great deal of firmness and courage of conviction went with his humility. His broad catholic attitude towards the religious beliefs of others is beyond question. He had respect for the followers of Shiva, Shri Krishna, Lord Buddha and Mahavir. He sincerely attempted a synthesis of the various schools of Indian philosophy. But he adhered firmly to his own experiences in the quest for truth, truth as he saw it. All the storm raised by the Vaishnava Vairagis of Ayodhya or the persecution to which he was subjected by the Saivas of Kashi could not shake it.

There are many stories handed down by tradition about the man's goodness and the good turn he did to those in distress. Some of these, shorn of miracles and magic, throw interesting light on the man and his motives. There is the story of the Brahmin pilgrim who had committed a heinous crime in the eyes of the Shastras and come to Kashi for explanation. The custodians of the Shastras treated him as an outcaste but the good poet not only owned him but also partook of food served by him in the name of Shri Ram. There is another oft-repeated story that when he was told that Shri Ram himself stood guard over his house by night, he gave away all his belongings to the needy and the poor. This gives us an idea not only of his selflessness but also of his colossal faith, as Edwin Creaves has pointed out, in God's solicitude for his devotees.

He cared little for the accumulation of material wealth or public recognition. In fact, the good man behind that his physical ailments in his old age were somehow connected with his own shortcomings as a devotee.

Inspite of all the stories about the miracles he is said too have performed, there is good reason to believe that he himself had little use for superstition and hypocrisy of any kind. He condemned those who went to a shrine for a son or the restoration of their eye-sight or those who believed in ghosts and spirits or the pseudo yogis who talked about the invisible and the unknowable.

One of the most striking aspects of Tulsidas's personality is his keen sense of objective beauty. He reveals in the description of his blue coloured deity stressing a thousand details of the lotus eyes, the lotus feet, the pink palms and the yellow robes. The vignetts of Shri Ram and Sita whether of the wedding altar, or in the forests during exile, or on their throne in Ayodhya are the warp and woof of his Ramayana's in various meters. Form, colour, beauty sweetness and power are the qualities he sees in his Ram and the same qualities he extols in his writings. I am willing to acknowledge anyone as my guru, he says "who can expound knowledge without reference to ignorance; or describe light of the context of darkness or set forth the formless without reference to form".

There are no records of his private life either at Ayodhya or at Kashi. But he had an intense personal feeling both for the Saryu and the Ganga. A bath in the river was part of the routine of his daily life and the milk and fruit diet which he prescribed as good for the seeker could also have been his own favourite diet.

The title Goswami has struck to his name so persistently that it has been suggested that for some time at least he was the head of a seat known as "the place of Gosain Tulsidasji" near Lolark-kund in Kashi. If this was so, he must have been rather uncomfortable in his situation because he expressly regrets that he had become a Gosain and forgotten the even tenor of his life. He was certainly averse to the institutionalisation of his experiences as a devotee and a seeker.

Two of his pet diversions were music and astrology and it is not unlikely that he enjoyed a game of chess. With all his absorption in things of the spirit, he had a keen sense of humour. In his own gentle, subtle manner he would not spare the gods "who pose as altruists but are for ever scheming" or the lonely holy men who would have lots of feminine company as soon as Shri Ram arrives in the forests and turns the rocks into moon faced beautiest.

There are hints in his own writings and in the writings of others that he had a fair complexion and a fine presence. A picture believed to be a copy of one made in his own life time, and now in the possession of his friend Ganga Ram Joshi's successors at Prahlad Ghat, represents him as a rather lean and thin but self possessed man of religion.

A great deal of wide-ranging scholarship went with his saintliness and it is impossible to miss his close familiarity with the principal schools of Indian philosophy on the one hand and the literary tradition embodied in the works of Sanskrit and Prakrit poets on the other. But he wrote his learning lightly and, what is even more remarkable, he had a lively appreciation of the limitations of mere literary skill and intellectual sharpness. The way of knowledge is like the sword's edge "he would say", "and the pitfalls are many and difficult to avoid". The man skilled only in the use of words can neither apprehend reality nor rise above pain and suffering. Poetry, morality and scholarship are good in their spheres but all of them must be ministers of love. It is impossible to separate the love of God which he extols in his writings from the love of humanity. There is a deep strain of human in all his prayers to his God and in all his exhortations for the cultivation of the good life.

Four centuries have rolled by since Tulsidas wrote his Ramcharitṃanasa and if his message continues to have a hold on the minds and hearts of millions of his countrymen, it is because of its abiding value and inner vitality. It is a simple faith which he taught. "The love of Shri Ram is born", he said in a simple heart and reflected in simple speech and action. Religious devotion for him was a way of life and it was no devotion, if it did not transfer the life of the devotee and give him peace and the love of mankind. His main theme in his great epic is the victory of righteousness over the forces of darkness and evil. The weapons with which Shri Ram fights and wins are "courage and fortitude, discrimination and self-control, a mind calm and unruffled and a heart full of love and compassion". This is so positive and so much the essence of the Indian view of life that its appeal to the Indian mind has been direct and irresistible.

Tulsidas felt that great poetry must be simple and as easily accessible a boon for all as the waters of the Ganga which makes for his immense popularity with the masses. The common man responds naturally to the manner in which he poses human issues in the context of human situations as he has to face similar issues in real life. The impact of such guileless but purposeful writing could not but be immediate and powerful.

No other poet in Northern India has reflected more faithfully or more successfully the core of Indian thought and cultural tradition in his writings and none has left a more permanent impression on the evolution of the thought and cultural behaviour of the people over the centuries. This due to his deep concern for the human situation and complete freedom from sectarian affiliations. In an age in which most saints and thinkers of his stature would have thought of founding a sect or a school, he used all his gifts as a poet and a saint to arrive at a synthesis and harmonise view points. In his own persuasive manner, he did much for the promotion of emotional integration among his people and in the long run he was much more successful than crusaders.

The unit of the good society which he envisaged was the individual, and the ideal citizen of his kingdom of God was a man who was free not only from ignorance and ill-will but also from disease and want. He recognised that there was no curse greater than poverty and no duty higher than doing good to others. He had much respect for an ordered life and the established norms based on sound judgement and the accumulated wisdom of the race, but the way of life which he himself preached recognised no distinctions of caste, sex or station in life. He had little patience with mentors who talked jargon and confused men's minds.

One of his crowning achievements was that he dispelled the mist of pessimism and abstract speculations which darkened and developed the lives of his people and gave them a healthy and positive creed, the keynotes of which were hope, joy, faith and fulfilment.

It is only natural that in our own time, Mahatma Gandhi, a great admirer of Tulsidas and a kindred soul, found much in the poet's writings to renovate the human soul and restore the people's faith in their national destiny.

The End

A keen social conscience is also in evidence in many of these quatrains. The poet is moved by the sight of "the Ravana of poverty holding the world in his grip". He draws a graphic picture of people in dire distress asking one another, "where shall we go? What shall we do? because the farmers have no fields to cultivate, the beggars get no alms, the businessmen have no vocation and servicemen seek jobs in vain. He observes that people in all ranks of society resort to questionable and immoral devices to keep body and soul together and arrives at the conclusion that "there are no fires more devastating than the fire of hunger". He is unhappy because people have given up the right path laid down by the Shastras and all sorts of new fangled beliefs hold the field. The misery, vice and poverty he saw all around him and the confusion created in men's minds by the so-called religious men seem to have persuaded him that there is no religion for man higher than the service of his fellow-men.

The Vinaya Patrika ranks only with the Ram-Charit-Manas as one of the crowning glories of the works of Tulsidas. It is a collection of lyrical songs. In the epic, the poet had to express his love for Shri Ram through the speech and action of others and the purposes of successful characterisation and dramatisation had to be met first. The general reader could see the deeper aspects of the poet's message of love only as through a glass darkly. In the Vinaya Patrika, which is in a real sense a sort of a spiritual biography, the poet is face to face with his Maker. He gives here, with fascinating candour and great intensity of feeling, a record of his endeavours to discover reality and the true nature of the way of love. This has led to a widespread but mistaken belief that it is some sort of a philosophical treatise in verse. His intensely personal, intimate approach, sincerity of fealing and the lyrical quality of the songs, make it one of the finest collections of devotional verses in all literature.

The story goes that when Kali found that the life and works of Tulsidas were weaning people away from him and making inroads on his own domains, he threatened the poet with dire consequences. The good god Hanuman advised the poet to present a petition in the court of Shri Ram. Both the title and the concluding verses of the collection lend colour to the story. But apart from the story, the feeling which inspires the poet, that he is laying bare his heart at the feet of his Master, helps both to organise the songs and to give them their unique devotional flavour. Each poem is a human record of the poet's struggle with the flesh and the devil, his attempts to solve the riddle of the universe, his eagerness to get into touch with the sources of light, peace and joy and the conclusions he arrives at gives us valuable hints both about him mature convictions and his inner personality. He finds that there is an all-pervading divinity "in the beginning, the middle and the end. To get into touch with it is the greatest opportunity of human life. Mere intellectual discussion is of little use here. It will not help a man to see light if he only sits enveloped in the darkness of a closed room by night and talks endlessly about a lamp and its light. If man could conquer anger, greed and ignorance he could see light. But it is not so easy to conquer them asceticism, austerities, elaborate rites and rituals are the ways suggested, but it is like making a rope of dust to bind down an elephant. Love, faith and surrender to the will of a Master who is full of compassion for the lowliest and the vilest are the only way.

The spontaneous feeling, the deep personal note, the unity and concentration of thought which we seek in the great lyric are all there in the songs of spiritual self-surrender collected in the Vinaya Patrika. There is no other work in which the authentic voice of the poet is to be heard more directly and distinctly.

Two calamities which overtook Kashi in his old age moved Tulsidasji deeply. These were the famine and the great plague. It was during the reign of Mughal Emperor Jahangir (A.D. 1605-1629) when the Punjab was in the grip of a deadly plague for so many years. This disease also spread to Agra where it remained for eight long years. Tuzuk-e-Jahangir has given detailed description of the havoc caused by it. Goswami Tulsidasji has also mentioned in his book entitled 'Kavitavali' that in the Bisi of Visvanatha a great grief had very badly overshadowed the town of Kashi. Contemporary records have also maintained that the plague broke out in Agra in the year 1616 but from the manner the poet associates the epidemic with an astrologically evil period called 'Meen ki Sanichari', it would appear that it visited Kashi even earlier. There is a note of deep misery over the plight of fellow-citizens in the powerfully objective picture of the havoc caused which the poet has drawn. He prays to his gods to spare Kashi for the city of Shankar had turned into a city of the dead and the dying. Tulsidasji has described in his verses the sufferings caused by this fatal and dreaded disease and pleaded with Mother Annapurana and Hanuman to have mercy on residents of Kashi and free the city from this disease. He also plead his Master, 'O Shri Rama, save us ! O Hanuman, save us!

In the verses of Hanuman Bahuka (Shloka 36-38) Tulsidasji has mentioned about his ailment as mentioned below:

रामगुलाम तुही हनुमान गुसाईं सुसाईं सुसाईं सदा मनुकूलो।
पाल्यौं हों बाल ज्यों आखर दू पितुमातु ज्यों मंगलमोद क्षमूलो।।
बाँह की बेदन, बाँहपगार! पुकारत आरत आनंद भूलो।
श्री रघुबीर निवारिफ पीर, रही दरबार परो लटी लूलो।।३६

काल की करालता, करमकठिनाई की धों,
पाप के प्रभाव, की सुभाय बाप बाबरे।
बेदन कुभाँति सो सही न जाति राति–दिन,
सोई बाँह गही जो गही समीर–डावरे।।
लयो तरु तुलसी निहारो, सो निहारि बारि,
सोचिए मलीन यो, तयो है तिहुँ ताब रे।
भूतनि की, आपनी, पराई हे कृपानिधान !
जानियत सबही की रीति राम रावरे।।३६

पाँय पीर, पेट–पीर, बाहु–पीर, मुँह पीर,
जरजर सकल सरीर पीरमई है।
देव, भूत, पितर, करम, खल, काल, ग्रह,
मोहिं पर दबरि दमानक सी दई है।।
हाँ तो बिन मोल ही बिकानो, बलि, बरि ही तें,
ओट रामनाम की ललाट लिखि लई है।
कुभंज के किकर बिकल बूड़े गोखुरनि,
हाय रामराय! ऐसी हाल कहूँ भई है।।३८।।

Tulsidas himself had a severe attack of plague and that was the cause of his death. The whole couplet of his poem is full of pleading of such a man who is undergoing great sufferings. He had mentioned that severe pain had set in his arm, the very arm by which Hanuman held him, probably the right one; then a gland appeared in the armpit, accompanied by fever, and afterwards pain spread over his whole body until it became unbearable.

In one place he says:

बालपने सूधे मन राम सनमुख भयो,
रामनाम लेत, माँगि खात टुकाटाक हों।
परयौ लोकरीति में, पुनीत प्रीति रामराम,
मोहबस बैठो तोरि तरिक तराक हौं।।
खोटे खोटे आचरण आचरत अपनाओ,
अंजनी कुमार, सोहयो रामपानि पाक हों।
तुलसी गुसाईं भयो, भोंड़े दिन भूलि गयो,
ताको फल पावत निदान परिपाक हो।।४०
असन–बसन हीन, विषम–विषाद–लीन,
देखि दीन दुबरो करे न हाय हाय को?
तुलसी अनाथ सो अनाथ रधुनाथ कियो,
दियो फल क्षीलसिंधु आपने सुभाय को।।
बीच यहि बीच पति पाइ भरुआइ गो,
बिहाय प्रभुभजन बचन मन काय को।
तातें तनु पेखियत धोर बरतीर मिस,
फूटि फूटि निकक्षत लीन रामराय को।।४२।।

"Once he was without food and clothing, week and poor, whosoever saw him in such a miserable condition, pited over him. This was the real picture of Tulsi before this period, there was nobody to help him or to look after him. In these circumstances, there was his only Master Shri Ram who looked after him. Tulsi further curse him that respect given to him by the common people after the blessing of Shri Ram he failed to digest that, he forget his Lord Shri Ram. He thought due this reason the salt of Shri Ram coming out from his body in the shape of a gland. In this couplet Tulsi feels that he is being punished for that pride and forgetfulness of Shri Ram.

In another stanza (38) of Hanuman Bhakta Tulsi said, There is a pain in the leg, pain the stomach, arm and face; the body is weak and old and full of pain; the gods, the spirits of the departed souls and the dead ancestors, time and the evil stars are all together attacking me as if they were firing cannon balls. In the last days of his life he was a most disgusted man on earth.... and says "Whatsoever I have sown I must reap". This turning of the search light inwards is so characteristic of the poet that it would be very farfetched to conclude that because his prayers were not answered, he lost all faith in divine intervention. Though after a long and painful illness Tulsidas recovered but failed to regain his vitality. In the year A.D. 1623 at the ripe age of near about 126 years (Samvat 1680) on the banks of the Ali Ganga (Kashi) on Saturday the third of the dark fortnight, in the month of Sravana, Tulsidas gave us his body. (July-August A.D. 1623 at the age of 125 years, 11 months and 7 days).

Baba Beni Madhav Das has mentioned in Mula Gosain Charit that at the time when Tulsi was approaching end, he had said,

> Having described the glory of Shri Rama,
> I am about to be silent,
> "Tulsi leaf and gold" will soon be put,
> in the mouth of Tulsi !

7

तुलसीदास जी के दोहे

Couplets of Tulsidasji
(Selection from Dohavalis)

पहले बनी प्रारब्ध, पाछे बना शरीर।
तुलसी यह आश्चर्य है, मन नहीं बांधे धीर।।

(Destiny was cast before body was born on finds,
Tulsi says it's a wonder no one is content in mind.

कर्म कमण्डलु कर गहै, तुलसी जहै लगि जाय।
सरिता सागर कूप जल, बूंद न अधिक समाय।।

Wherever one goes, says Tulsi,
One Carries the vessel of one's action;
Go to a river, well or sea,
Not a drop more can you carry fruition.

जग से छतीस होय रहो, राम चरण छः तीन।
तुलसी हिय वियारये, यह मतो परवीन।।

O ! Seeker ! In worldly life you should lie like the digit 36 where both the numerals remain with their backs towards each other, in other words, you should turn your back towards the world. But in spiritual life, your face should be towards the lotus feet of the Lord, just as in the digit 63, in which both the numerals face each other. Says Saint Tulsidas, this is the way, the wise should live i.e. with his face always turned towards the Lord.

जो कोई कहे सन्त हम चीन्हा।
तुलसी हाथ कान धरि लीन्हा।।

(If someone says that he has tested a Saint, Saint Tulsidas would put his hand on his ears out of remorse)

तुलसी कमलनि जल बसै, रवि ससि बसें अकास।
जो जाके मन में बसै, सो ताहि के पास।।

Saint Tulsidasji says that the flowers of Kumud (Asphodel) and Kamalni (Lotus) grow and abide in the water while the Sun and the Moon are in the sky. Inspite of this vast distance, the heart of these flowers is closely set on them. If attachments and devotion are possible despite such a distance, it is obvious that a thing which abides in one's heart and mind, it is with him whatever the distance.

All must have observed the flowers of Kumud and Kamalni. These are generally found in ponds and tanks. How surprising it is that flowers growing out of water should have such deep attachment with the Sun and the Moon. The characteristic of Kamal flower (lotus) is that it blossoms with the rising of the Sun and closes its petals when the Sun sets. On the other hand, the Kumudni flower (Asphodel) blossoms with the rising of the Moon and closes its petals when the Moon sets. The Kamal flower fades during the night and Kumudni flower during the day.

तुलसी इस संसार में, पाँच रत्न हैं सार।
साध संग सतगुरु शरण, दया दीन उपकार।।

Saint Tulsidasji says that there are five pricelesss and real gems in this world. These are : Company of the Saints, surrender to the Sadguru, mercy, humility and doing good to others.

He who possesses the priceless gems of mercy and humility is wealthy. Therefore, there should be peace in the mind and sweetness in words. One should harbour good will towards all so that one may live in peace himself and bestow the same on others as well.

तुलसी मीठे बचन ते, सुख उपजन चहूँ ओर।
बशीकरण यह मन्त्र है, परिहर बचन कठोर।।

Tulsi says words sweet dispense comfort on sides all,
Sweetness wins hearts, roughness annoys big and small.

मोल चतुर्दश भुवन को, एक श्वास है तोहि।
ऐसे धन रघुनाथ को, तुलसी वृथा न खोहि।।

The value of your breath is equal to the wealth of fourteen Bhawanas (celestial mansions), therefore do not waste such a precious breath.

चित्रकूट सब दिन वसत, प्रभु सिय–लषन–समेत।
रामनाम–जय जापकहिं, तुलसी अभिमत देत।।

(The Lord with Lakshmana and Sita in Chitrakut for ever lives,
To those who take His Holy name what they desire in life He gives.)

पय अहार फल खाइ जपु रामनाम षर मास।
सकल सुमंगल सिद्धि सब करतल तुलसीदास।।

Shri Rama's Name repeat for half a year and then on milk and fruits remain,
Tulsi all welfare shall be yours, His Bounty you shall soon attain.

रामनाम–मनि दीप धरु जीह–देहरी द्वार।
तुलसी भीतर वाहिरी जो चाहसि उजियार।।

(On tongue, the door-still of your heart, place lamp of Rama's Name dazzling bright,
Says Tulsi, both within without, if you seek keen discernments light.)

रामनाम को अंक है, सब साधन है सुन।
अंक गए कछु हाथ नहिं, अंक रहे दसगुन।।

(Like numeral is the Name of Rama, all other means are like a naught,
The numeral gone nothing remains, tenfold it turns effort that was).

कासी विधि बस तनु तजे, हढि तन तजे प्रयाग।
तुलसी जो फल सो सुलभ रामनाम अनुराग।।

(Praying in Kashi who breathes his last, in Prayag who is consigned,
Tulsi says, fruits which one attains, with ease in the Name of Shri Ram one finds).

मीठो अरु कठवति भरो, रीताई अरु खेम।
स्वास्थ परमारथ सुलभ, रामनाम के प्रेम।।

(If you seek boul of nectar sweet, king's glory with calm grace retained,

Selfish aims and salvation too these are by love in Shri Rama's Name gained).

स्वास्थ सुख सपनेहुँ अगम परमारथ न प्रबेस।
रामनाम सुमिरत मिटहिं तुलसी कठिन कलेस।।

(Lacking earth's comfort's seen in dreams and bliss of Heaven denied,

Those who depend on the Name of Shri Rama, free from all woes in world reside).

बिगरी जनम अनेक को सुधरे अबही आजु।
होहि राम को, नाम जपु, तुलसी जति कुसमाज।।

(In the cycles of life and death, you have dwelt, arise to save your lot today,

Tulsidas says, repeat the name of Shri Ram, renounce it for ever evil's way).

प्रीति प्रतीति सुरीति सों रामनाम जपु राम।
तुलसी तेरो है भलो आदि मध्य परिनाम।।

(love, devotion and with faith, repeat the gracious Name of Shri Ram,

Tulsi says' good fortune will be yours, today in past and future deeds).

बरषाऋतु रघुपति–भगति तुलसी सालि सुदास।
रामनाम वर वरन जुग सावन भादों मास।।

(Devotee of God are like paddy fields, Devotion is like monsoon rains,

Tulsi is like Sawan-Bhadon, Like two letters of Shri Rama's Holy Name.

रामनाम कलि कामतरु सकल सुमंगल कदं।
सुमिरत करतल सिद्धि सब पग पग परमानंद।।

(Wish bearing Tree is the Name of Shri Ram, Devotion is like plenty's cow

In Kali Yug root of all welfare is guru's holy feet to bow.

सकल कामनाहीन जो रामभगति–रसलीन।
नाम प्रेम–पीयुष–हद तिनहूँ किए मन मीन।।

(Those who had controlled their desires, in Shri Rama's devotion who are steeped,
In the sea of Nectar of Shri Rama's Name, like sporting fish their minds they keep)

रामनाम पर राम तें प्रीति प्रतीति भरोस।
सो तुलसी सुमिरत सकल सगुन सुमंगल कोस।।

(Who with love and faith depend on Shri Rama's Holy Name,
Tulsi says, need only dwell upon the Name of Shri Rama wealth of all welfare to attain)

तुलसी प्रीति प्रतीति सों रामनाम–जप जाग।
किए हीय विधि दाहिनो देइ अभागेहि भाग।।

(With devotion of deep love and faith the Holy Name of Shri Ram whosoever take,
Tulsi says, their woes and sufferings God ends and turns into good fortune).

जल थल नभ गति अमित अति, अग जग जीव अनेक।
तुलसी तोसे दीन कहें, रामनाम गति एक।।

(Various creature remain moving from water, air, soil and sky,
O Tulsi ! helpless in your life, in Shri Rama's Name You would fixed remain).

राम भरोसे, राम बल, रामनाम विस्वास।
सुमिरत सुभ मंगल कुसल माँगत तुलसीदास।।

(May strength be Shri Ram and faith be Shri Ram,
Shri Ram's shelter only Tulsi seeks,
The Name which spells welfare and joy,
That Name alone Tulsi beseeches;

रामनाम रति, राम गति रामनाम विस्वास।
सुमिरत सुभ मंगल कुसल, दुहुँ दिसि तुलसीदास।।

(Those who have firm faith, love and affection in the Name of Shri Ram,

Tulsi says, they will get everything on earth in the Name of Shri Ram).

रे मन! सब सो निरस ह्वँ सरस राम सों होहि।
भलो सिखावन देत है निसि दिन तुलसी तोहि।।

(Oh ! my mind, renounce attachment from all, devotion deep in Shri Rama's Feetlay,
This is Tulsi's true advice, repeating firmly night and day).

हरे चरहिं, तापहिं वरत, फेर पसारहि हाथ।
तुलसी स्वारथ मीत सब, परमारथ रघुनाथ।।

(People tend young saplings for their needs;
fruit, firewood, fodder from their leaves,
Tulsi says, that people give to something take;
from Shri Ram sans giving one receives).

स्वारथ सीताराम सों, परमारथ सियराम।
तुलसी तेरो दूसरे द्वार कहा कहु काम।।

(Sita-Rama grants your earthly wants,salvation too Sita-Rama give,
Tulsi says, why most then you seek another door a while you live?)

स्वारथ परमारथ सकल सुलभ एक ही ओर।
द्वार दूसरे दीनता उचित न तुलसी तोर।।

(When both salvation and your requirements, with Shri Rama's devotion you can get,
Tulsi says, needless is your quest at doors of other lords to beg).

तुलसी स्वारथ रामहित, परमारथ रघुवीर।
सेवक जाके लषन से पवनपूत रनधीर।।

(For you Tulsi, your hopes on earth and for salvation in Rama rest,
Shri Rama who had devotees great like Lakshmana, Hanuman warrior best).

राम सनेही, राम गति, रामचरन रति जाहि।
तुलसी फल जगु–जनम को दियो विधाता ताहि।।

(Whose love is Shri Rama and life is Shri Rama, who is devotee of Shri Rama's Feet,
Tulsi, on him God has bestowed the fruits of birth in life to reap).

आपू आपने ते अधिक जेहि प्रिय सीताराम।
तेहिक पग की पानहीं, तुलसी–तनु को चाम।।

(More than themselves than their own who Sita-Rama with deep love seek,
Tulsi his skin would gladly give to them for shoes to clad their feet).

स्वारथ परमारथ रहित सीताराम–सनेह।
तुलसी सो फल चारि को फल हमार मत एह।।

(Those who seek not moksha nor earthly gains, for Sita-Rama with deep love seek,
Tulsi his skin would gladly give to them for shoes to clad their feet).

जे जन रखे विषयरस, चिकने रामसनेह।
तुलसी ते प्रिय राम के, कानन बसहिं कि गेह।।

(Those who are in Shri Rama's devotion steeped sense pleasures having cast aside,
Tulsi, unto Rama they are dear, whether in home or woods abide).

तुलसी श्री रघुबीर तजि करे भरोसो और।
सुख संपति की का चली नरकहु नाही रौर।।

(Tulsi, if one has turned from Shri Rama, in other hopes has sought to dwell,
Futile are thoughts of wealth and peace, he cannot enter even hell).

तुलसी हरि अपमान तें होइ अकाज समाज।
राज करत रज मिलि गए सदल सकुल करुराज।।

(Tulsi who bears Hari insult, welfare to evil fate doth yield,
Like Duryodhana with kins he lies midst dust; upon life's battle field).

एक भरोसो, एक बल, एक आस विस्वास।
एक राम–घनश्याम हिल चातक तुलसीदास।।

(One is my hope, one is my strength, in one is my reliance faith,
For one drop from Rama's sky blue form, like chatak Tulsi always awaits).

नीच निचाई नहिं तजै सज्जन हु के संग।
तुलसी चंदन–बिरप बसि बिनु बिष भए न भुअंग।।

(If evil men good company seek, their vile nature they cannot hide,
Like snakes who poison cannot leave even if on sandal they abide).

भलो भलाई पे लहै, लहै निचाई नीचु।
सुधा सराहिय अमरता, गरल सराहिय मीचु।।

(The righteous follow virtue's path, the wicked choose to dwell in vice,
Nectar is praised for giving health, poison for bringing end to life).

मिश्या माहुर सज्जनहिं, खलहिं गरल सम साँच।
तुलसी छुवत पराई ज्यों पारद पावक–आँच।।

(For wicked Truth like poison is, Falsehood for saints does venom spell,
From Truth flee vide, virtuous from lies, like fire does mercury dispel).

रामचन्द्र–मुख चन्द्रमा चित चकोर जब होइ।
रामराज सब काज सुभ समय सुहावन सोइ।।

(To gaze on moon like face of Shri Rama like Chakor when mind stead fast yearns,
All welfare does then one attend, like Reign of Rama that moment turns).

मनि मानिक महँगे किए, सहँगे तृन, जल, नाज।
तुलसी एतो जानिए राम गरीब–नेवाज।।

(Rubies and gems God hath made scarce; grass, water, grains in plenty gives,
Tulsi says, from this you should know, Rama shelters one who forlon lives).

तुलसी 'ममता राम सों' समता सब संसार।
राग न रोष न दोष दुख, दास भए भवपार।।

(Tulsi, who bear true love for Shri Rama all in the world alike who treat,
Who have no hatred, wish none ill, from life-death cycles they are freed).

तुलसी वेद–पुरान–मत, पूरन सास्त्र बिचार।
यह बिराग–संदीपिनी अखिल ज्ञान को सार।

(Is the essence of knowledge,
The views of Vedas and Puranas,
The ideas of all the Shastras,
Are contained in it.

(Describing the merit of his book, "The Vairagya Sandipani" Tulsidasji said the above couplet).

17-VS/ सील गहनि सबकी सहनी, कहनी हीय मुख राम।
81 Handoo तुलसी रहिए एहि रहनि, सन्त जनन को काम।।

(Those who accept (the path of) morality
And forbear with all;
Those who from heart and mouth,
Repeat always Shri Rama,
To live in this manner,
Tulsi says,
Is the way of the holy ones)

23-VS/ तन करि मन करि बचन करि, काहू दूषित नाहिं।
81 Handoo तुलसी ऐसे संतजन, रामरूप जग माहि।।

(Those who in by body, mind and word
Do not find faultwith others,
Tulsi says, such holy ones,
Are the (living forms of Rama
In the World).

23-VS/ मुख देखत पातक हरै, परसत कार्य बिलाहि।
81-Handoo बचन सुनत मन मोहगत, पूरव भाग मिलाहि।।

(At the sight of such a one's face one's sins disappear,
By touching him Karmas are destroyed
Hearing his words delusion is lost,
One meets such a saint
By the merit of past good deeds

53-VS/ अंहकार की अगिनि में, दहत सकल संसार।
P-82 Handoo तुलसी बाँचे संतजन, केवल साति अधार।

Comparing peace to water and ego to fire,
Tulsi says:-
The whole world burns
In the fire of the ego,
Tulsi says, the holy one,

To saved by holding on
To peace alone?

55-VS/ तेज होत तन तरनि को अचरज मानत लोइ।
P-82 Handoo तुलसी जो पानी भया, बहुरि न ग्रावक होइ।।

(The radiance of his body
Is like the sun,
People are astonished
When they see him,
He who has become water
Can never again, says Tulsi,
Be turned into fire).

Dohavali रामनाम–मनि--दीप धरू जीह--देहरी द्वार।
6/93 Handoo तुलसी भीतर बाहिरी जो चाहसि उजियार।।

(If you wish to have inner and outer illumination,
keep the jewel lamp of the name of Rama.
On the threshold of your tongue, says Tulsi).

D.7/ हिय निर्गन, नयनन्हि सगुन, रसना राम सुनाम।
93 Handoo मनहुँ पुरट–संपुट लसत, तुलसी ललित ललाम।।

(Let the God with attributes
Dwell in the heart,
The God with attributes in the eyes,
Keep the blessed name on your lips.
By doing so, says Tulsi, you will have
A precious stone in a beautiful box of gold).

D.8/ सगुन ध्यान रूचि सरस नहि, निर्गन मन ते दूरि।
P.93 Handoo तुलसी सुमिरहु राम को नाम सजीवन–मूरि।।

(Distasteful is meditation on the qualified God,
The unqualified is also far from the mind,
Then, says "Tulsi', remember,
The life giving name of Rama")

D.251/ ज्ञान कहै असान बिनु तम बिनु कहै प्रकास।
P.94 Handoo निरगुन कहे जो सगुन बिनु सो गुरू तुलसीदास।।

(He is my teacher, says Tulsi,
'Who can explain,
The unqualified without the qualified
or knowledge without ignorance
And light without darkness).

D.252/ अंक अगुन, आखर सगुन, सामझि उभय प्रकार।
P.94 Handoo खोए राखे आपु भल, तुलसी चारू विचार।।

The Nirguna is like numbers,
The Saguna is like words,
Tulsi says, 'understand both',
Then reject or accept).

D.563/ स्रवन घटहु, पुनि दग घटहु, घटहु सकल बल देह।
P.95 Handoo इते धरे घटि है कहा जो न धरै हरि–नेह?।।

(The powers of hearing and seeing may decrease,
The strength of the whole body may fail,
But what will this loss amount to,
If the love of God remains constant).

D.252/ अंक अगुन आखर सगुन सामझि उभय प्रकार।
P.96 Handoo खोए राखे आपु भल, तुलसी चारू विचार।।

(Affection may be tested in three successive ways,
And enmity in the reverse order.
The best, the mediocre and the poor (in friendship)
May be compared with stone, sand and water
respectively).

D.468/ पुरूषारथ, पूरब करम, परमेश्वर पर धान।
P.96 Handoo तुलसी पैरत सरित ज्यों सवहिं काज अनुमान।।

(It is good to run away in (case of) attack.
It is also good to strike in self defence.
But it is never good to injure anyone in return.
Tulsi says, Rama is there alone all to protect us).

In verse number 571 of Dohavali, Tulsidasji describes the merit that may be gained by the study of his book:

D.571/ मनिमय दोहा दीप जहें, उर घर प्रकट प्रकास।
P.97 Handoo तहँ न मोह भय–तम तमी, कलि कज्जली विलास।।

(The darkness of delusion,
The night of fear,
The soot (impurity) of Kali
Can have no sway,
When the jewel lamp of these verses
Lights up the home of the heart).

(258) तुलसी अदभुत देवता आसादेवी नाम।
सेए सोक समपंई, विमुख भए अभिराम।।

(Tulsi says,
The goddess named Hope
is a strange deity.
She rewards service
with sorrow and
opposition with happiness).

(468) पुरूषारथ, पूरव करम, परमेश्वर परधान।
तुलसी पैरत सरित ज्यों सवहिं काज अनुमान।।

Like the support to a swimmer in crossing the river,
All undertakings may be accomplished in three ways,
They are self-effort and past karmas (inherited in the form of tendencies)
But the most important is the grace of God).

(468) ज्ञान कहे अज्ञान बिनु, तम बिनु कहै प्रकास।
निरगुन कहै जो सगुन बिनु सो गुरू, तुलसीदास।।

(He is my teacher, says Tulsidas
'Who can explain,
The unqualified without the Qualified
or Knowledge without ignorance
And light without darkness).

(252) अंक अगुन आखर सगुन सामझि उभय प्रकार।
खोए राखे आपु भल, तुलसी चारू विचार।।

(The Nirguna is like numbers,
The Saguna is like words,

Tulsi says, understand both;
Then reject or accept.)

(563) स्रवन घटहु, पुनि दृग घटहु, घटहु सकल बल देह।
इते धरे घटि है कहा जो न धरै हरि–नेह?।।

(The power of hearing and seeing may decrease,
The strength of the whole body may fail,
But what will this loss amount to,
If the love of God remains constant.)

(6) रामनाम–मनि–दीप धरू जीह–देहरी द्वार।
तुलसी भीतर बाहिरी जो चाहसि उजियार।।

If you wish to have inner and outer illumination,
Keep the jewel lamp of the name of Rama
On the threshold of your toungs, says Tulsi)

(7) हिय निर्गुन, नयनन्हि सगुन, रसना राम सुनाय।
मनहुँ पुरट–संपुट लसत, तुलसी ललित ललाय।।

(Let the God without attributes
Dwell in the heart,
The God with attributes in the eyes,
Keep the blessed name on your lips.
By doing so, says Tulsi, you will have
A precious stone in a beautiful box of gold)

(8) सुगन ध्यान रूचि सरस नहि, निर्गुन मन ते दूरि।
तुलसी सुमिरहु राम को नाम सजीवन–मूरि।।

(Distasteful is meditation on the qualified God,
The unqualified is also far from the mind,
Then says Tulsi, remember,
The life giving name of Rama)

(424) भागे भल, आड़ेहु भलो, भलो न धाले धाउ।
तुलसी सबके सीस पर रखवारो रघुराउ।।

(It is good to run away in (case of) attack.
It is also good to strike in self defence.
But it is never good to injure anyone in return.
Tulsi says, Rama is there above all to protect us).

H.99/E.92 करमठ कठमालिया कहै, ज्ञानी ज्ञानविहीन।
तुलसी त्रिपथ विहाय गो, रामगुआरे दीन।।

(Tulsi says that Paths of action (Karamyoga), devotion (bhaktiyoga), Knowledge (Gyanyogya) are the three means of human pursuit for salvation. He also says that he is unaware of these paths. He only wants Shri Rama's mercy).

H.105/E.97 राम निकाई रावरी है सब ही को नीक।
जो यह साँची है सदा तो नीको तुलसीक।।

(O Rama ! the pleasure of Thy will
Spells welfare for all born on earth,
If it is true always, Tulsi is of the opinion,
there is no death of welfare on earth).

H.100/98 बाधक सब सब के भए, साधक भय न कोई
तुलसी राम कृपालु तें भलो हुइ सो होइ।।

(Rough paths of life are full of pits,
support indeed is hard to find
Tulsi, welfare one gets on earth when
Gracious Rama is so inclined).

H.75/E.99 तुलसी उद्यम करम जग जब जेहि राम सुडीठि।
होइ सुफल सोइ, ताहि सब सनमुख प्रभु तन पीठि।।

(Tulsi says, efforts, fates only bear fruits
When Shri Ram bestows His grace
All attachments then said and one
beholds Shri Rama's face).

H.106/E 100 तुलसी राम जो आदरयो खोटो खरो खरोइ।
दीपक काजर सिर धरयो, धरचो सु धरयो धरोइ।।

(Tulsi says, to whom Shri Rama gives mercy,
Worthy or not, into worth turns
Lamp, holds black soot over its flames
forming collyrium as it burns).

H.136/E 104 कहहिं विमलमति संत, वेद पुरान विचारि अस।
द्रवै जानकीकंत तब छुटै संसार दुख।।

(According to the wise saints that All the

Vedas and Puranas are full of the advice
that one can only get rid of earthly woes
when only Shri Rama have mercy on them).

H.149/E 105 तुलसी जाने सुनि समझि कृपासिंधु रघुराज।
महँगे मनि कंचन किए, सौंधे जग, जल नाज।।

(Tulsi is fully aware that Shri Rama is a
ocean of Mercy he knows
He has made gold and gems costly, but
grain and water freely flows).

बालक कोसलपाल के सेवक पाल कृपाल।
तुलसी मन–मानस बसत मंगल मंजु मराल।।

(Child Rama, sweet son of Kaushal's Lord,
save devotees mercy takes,
Such Rama abides in Tulsi's heart,
like graceful swan sporting in lake)

H.152/E.136 सुधे मन, सूधे वचन सूधी सब करतूति।
तुलसी सुधी सकल विधि रघुवर–प्रेम–प्रसूति।।

(Whose heart is simple, speech is sweet,
whose actions are gentle and kind.
Tulsi, always Rama's love to get such
virtuous ones with ease will find).

H/181/E.137 होहुँ कहावत, सब कहत, राम सहत उपहास।
साहब सीतानाथ से, सेवक तुलसीदास।।

(Tulsi is Rama's devotees called, to presume
Tulsi too, dares, Even Sita's Lord with mercy
moved this just with patient humour bears).

H.129/E.158 श्री रघुवीर– प्रताप तें सिध तरे पाषान।
ते मतिमंद जे राम तजि भजहिं जाय प्रभू आन।।

(By Mercy of the gracious Rama, rocks floated on waters
of seas,
Foolish indeed is one who turns from such a Lord and
others seek).

H.107/E.170 तनु विचित्र, कायर बचन, अहि अहार, मन घोर।
तुलसी हरि भए परछधर ताते कह सब मोर।।

(Of unique body, lazy speech, on snakes
hard hearted peacocks dine,
Lord sports their feathers midst his curls,
Tulsi so mortals call them Mine).

H.116/E.217 सुद्ध सच्चदानंदमय कंद भानु– कुलकेतु।
चरित करत नर अनुहरत संसृति–सागर–सेतु।।

(O Pure ! O Truth ! Consciousness ! Bliss ! Banner
of Surya's Clan ! Gracious Rama !
Thy seeds for mortals are like bridge to
make over life's sea crossing calm).

H.101/E.218 संकरप्रिय मम द्रोही, सिवद्रोही मम दास।
ते नर करहिं कलप भरि घोर नरक महं वास।।

(Lord said: 'Who love Shiva, oppose Me;
or regard Me but Shiva despise,
Such mortals for a full Kalpa shall in Hells
eternal fire reside').

H.89/E.223 नातो नाते राम के, रामसनेह सनेहु।
तुलसी मांगत जोरि कर जनम जनम सिब देहु।।

(With folded hands Tulsi begs Thee,
O Shiva grant him this humble prayer;
All bonds for Tulsi be through Rama, for
Rama alone love he may bear)

H.241/E.224 और करे अपराध कोउ, और पाव फल–भोग।
अति विचित्र भगवंतगति, कोउ न जानिवे जोग।।

(Misdeeds and vices some commit, while others
trials and sufferings bear,
Mysterious is the will of God, to comprehand
it does one fare)?

H.177/E.233 काल करम गुन दोष जग जीव तिहरि हाथ।
तुलसी रघुवर रावरो, जान जानकीनाथ।।

(In Thy Hand rests all action time qualities
faults, life and its fate
O Sita's Lord ! Tulsi is Thine ! accept him
and Thine own him make).

H.273/E.234 कहत कठिन, समुझत कठिन, साधत कठिन विवेक।
होइ धुनाक्षरन्याय जौ, पुनि प्रत्यूह अनेक।। (273)

(Terse to expound and to imbibe, hard is the
Path knowledge doth preach,
And if perchance it is attained, obstacles ere goal we
reach)?

H.251/E.235 ज्ञान कहै अज्ञान बिनु तम बिनु कहै प्रकास।
निरगुन कहै जो सगुन बिनु सो गुरू तुलसीदास।।

(Passion, greed, anger brother dear, all these are
forms of vilest vice,
Beware ! they may in moments few even
mind of greatest sage entice).

H.98/E.236 जाने जानत जोइये, बिनु जाने को जान?।
तुलसी यह सुनि समुझि, हिय आनु धरे धनुवान।।

(Formless knowledge elusive is,
few seeking can ere hope to find,
Says Tulsi, dwell upon this well,
Rama with bow arrow bring in mind).

H.90/E.23 सब साधन को एक फल, जेहि जान्यो सोइ जान।
ज्यों त्यों मन–मंदिर बसहिं राम धरे धनु वान।।

(The wise indeed is one who knows of all efforts one is aim,
Whatever be the means, in heart Rama with bow arrows
may remain).

H.137/E.238 बिन गुरू होई कि ज्ञान, ज्ञान कि होइ बिराग बिनु?।
गावहि वेद पुरान, सुख कि लहिय हरिभगति बिनु।।

(Sans guru can one learn?
Can knowledge sans detachment be?
Lasting peace none can earn,
save by Devotion, thus Vedas sing).

H.484/E.239 फूलै फरै न बेत, जदपि सुधा वरषहिं जलद।
मूरख हृदय न चेत, जो गुरू मिलैं विरंचि सिव।।

(Even if clouds nectar rain,
Cane bush will not fruit blossoms bear,
Guru like Brahma may train,
but hearts attached shall knowledge lack).

H.138/E.240 रामचन्द्र के भजन बिनु जो यह पद निर्वान।
ज्ञानवंत अपि सोइ नर पसु बिनु पुँछ विखान।।

(Those who bless of salvation seek yet songs of
Rama to sing they fail,
Inspite of learning helpless are like beasts who
lose their horns or tail).

H.252/E.241 अंक अगुन, आखर सगुन, सामझि उभय प्रकार।
खोए राखे आपु भल, तुलसी चारू विचार।।

(Of Nirguna-Saguna natuare know, like
numerals, figures, same apart,
In which his welfare this decide, says Tulsi,
then take one to heart).

H.326/E.258 तुलसी बैर सनेह दोउ रहित बिलोचन चारि।
सुरा सवेरा आदरहिं, निदहिं सुरसरि–बारि।।

(Tulsi, both Love and Hate are blind, without
discernment wisdom fails,
Like Tantrik Ganga's water scorns, but wine
with zealous fervour hails).

H.254/E.266 सोई सेवँर तेइ सुवा, सेवा सदा बसंत।
तुलसी महिमा मोह की सुनत सराहत संत।।

(Dry pods on cotton trees each spring parrots
Persist pecking in vain,
Such is attachment's power Tulsi, seeing which
Sages in awe remain).

H.535/E.320 उखी परि कलहीन होद, उपर कलाप्रधान।
तुलसी देखु कलापगति, साधन–धन पहिचान।।

(True love when nature borne Tulsi,
ceases not even when one dies,
Behold the rootless mayur shrub sprouts
c'en as clouds thunder in skies).

H.408/E.328 बचन बेष क्यों जानिए, मन मलीन नर नारि।
सूपनखा, मृग पूतना, दसमुख प्रमुख बिचारि।।

(From outward show of speech and form can one
low hearts of mortals find?
Bring Ravana, Maricha, Srupnakha and Putana's
conduct to your mind).

H.489/E.341 जो सुनि समुझि अनीतिरत, जागत रहे जु सोई
उपदेसिबो जगाइवो तुलसी उचित न होई।।

(Who grasps all things of them aware yet heart
in ways of vice has lain,
He seems awake, yet is asleep to wake him
Tulsi, is in vain).

H.368/E.357 होइ भले के अनभलो, होइ दानि के सूम।
होइ कुपूत सुपूत के, ज्यों पावक में धूम।।

(As smoke arises from pure fire,
so evil may from virtue grow
To generous may be thrifty born,
wayward son wealth of worthy throw).

H.536/E.363 तुलसी संगत पोच की सुजनहि होत मदानि।
ज्यों हरि रूप सुताहि ते कीन गुहारो आनि।।

(Despite vile company virtuous men,
to welfare soon are surely led,
Tulsi, Lord came when Princess called,
who had to Vishnu's form been wed).

H.363/E.364 राम–कृपा तुलसी सुलभ गंग सुसंग समान।
जो जल परै जो जन मिलै, कीजै आपु सामान।।

(Bliss of Ganga and saint's company is same,
Tulsi by grace of Rama,

As waters cannot Ganga taint, vile men cannot
good company harm).

H.532/E.365 बड़ो गहे ते होत बड़, ज्यों बावन–कर दंड।
श्री प्रभु के संग सों बढ़ो, गयो अखिल ब्रह्माड़।।

(Company of great men greatness gives,
like staff of Lord in Vamna form,
As Lord in all the three worlds stepped,
staff too did journey great perform).

H.364/E.366 ग्रह, भेषज, जल, पवन, पर, पाइ कुजोग सुजोग।
होइ कुबस्तु सुवस्तु जग, लखहि सुलच्छन लोग।।

(Water and wind, shelter and dress, are good
and bad in different modes,
Those who can calmly thus reflect get peace
on life's hazardous roads).

H.341/E.386 सुकृत न सुकृति परिहरै, कपट न कपटी नीच।
मरत सिरवान देइ चले, गीधराज मारीच।।

(The unkind leaves not guile till death,
the kind for good over strives,
Truth of this precept had been shown when
Marich, Jatayu lay their lives).

H.447/E.410 तुलसी असमय के सखा धीरज, धर्म विवेक।
साहित, साहस, सत्यव्रत, राम भरोसो एक।।

(Tulsi in distress these are friends; patience;
discernment, books of dharma,
Courage unswerving path of Truth,
towards Rama to look steadfast and firm).

H.533/E.418 तुलसी दान जो देत है जल में हाथ उठाय।
प्रतिग्राही जीवै नहीं, दाता नरकै जाय।।

(Who raises hands to offerings make,
Tulsi, in waters fish to net,
Who take the offerings do not live,
he himself too Hell's woes shall get).

H.486/E.421 अनसमुझे, अनूसोचनो, अवसि समुझिए आपु।
तुलसी आपु न समझिए पलपल पर परितापु।।

(What you cannot first understand,
reflect and it will then be known,
What you cannot by yourself grasp,
to grief each moment will be prove).

H.329/E.429 सदा न जे सुमिरत रहहिं, मिलि न कहहिं प्रिय बैन।
तेपै तिन्हके जाहिं घर जिनके हियै न नैन।।

(Memories in whom do not abide,
who does not with kind words receive,
To him goes only such a one who call
of love cannot perceive).

H.330/E.432 हित पुनीत सब स्वारथहिं, अरि असुद्ध बिनु चाड़।
निज मुख मानिक सम दसन, भूमि परे ते हाड़।।

(What served self as worthy and pure,
unwanted worthless harmful grows,
Like tooth dislodged is bone unclean,
Which was like mani set in rows).

H.371/E.433 जो जो जेहि जेहि रस मगन तहँ सो मुदित मन मानि।
रस गुन दोष विचरिवो रसिकरीति पहिचानि।।

(Of longings which are dear to heart,
in their fulfilment joy one finds,
But of their qualities being aware signs of
wrapt discerning minds).

H.495/E.434 तुलसी भेड़ी की धँसनि जड़–जनता सनमान।
उपजत की अभिमान भो, खोवत मूढ़ अपान।।

(Support of rustic masses weak is like that
of a herd of sheep,
Foolish turn proud when thus acclaimed,
their minds discernment do not keep).

H.372/E.435 सम प्रकास–तम पारव दुहुँ, नामभेद विधि कीन्ह।
ससि पोषक सोषक समझि जग जस अपजस दीन्ह।।

(Alike are both halves of the moon,
same are its dark and moonlit nights
Moon's waxing half bright honour brings,
its waving half moon's repute slights).

H.328/E.439 अमिय गिरि गारेउ गरल, गारि कीन्ह करतार।
प्रेम बैर की जननि जुग, जानहिं बुध, न गवाँर।।

(Hard spoken words the creator made of both,
nectar and poisson strain,
From them both love discord are born,
this know the wise and not the plain).

H.496/E.463 लही आँख कब आँधर, बाँझ पूत कब ल्याय?
कब कोढ़ी काया लही? जग बहराइच जाइ।।

(To Bahraich all in fervour rush,
but who to ask himself has passed,
Has one gained sight, been blest with child,
or leper's skin has healing caused).

H.355/E.478 तुलसी अपनो आचरन भलो न लागत कासु।
तेहि न बसात जो खात नित लहसुनहू को बासु।।

(Says Tulsi, there is none indeed who thinks
his conduct to be wrong,
One who by habit garlic takes,
finds not its odour to be strong).

H.377/E.489 नीच निरावहिं निरस तरू, तुलसी सींचहि ऊख।
बरखि विस्व हरषित करत, हरत ताप अध त्यास।।

(While selfish mortals pull out weeds and
nurture sprouts of sugarcane,
The clouds give every shrub on earth an
equal measure of their rain).

H.481/E.490 तुलसी स्वास्थ सामुही, परमारथ तनु पीठि।
अंध कहै दुख पाइहो, डिठियारो केहि डीठि।।

(Tulsi, who looks to selfish ends and turning
from salvation flies,

To be called sightless hurts his heart
but how can one say he has eyes?)

H.487/E.492 कूप खनत मंदिर जरत, आए धारि बबूर।
बबहिं, नवहिं निज काज सिर कुमित–सिरोमनि कूर।।

(Who digs a well when his house burns
sows babul when his foes attack,
Who bows to all for selfish ends,
such lazy lead who wisdom lack).

H490/E.493 बहु मुख, बहु रूचि, बहु वचन, बहु आचार व्यवहार।
इनको भलो मनाइबो, यह अज्ञान अपार।।

(Too many children who desires,
Lazy whose ways, action and speech,
Dame Fortune such mortals eludes,
in folly they their welfare seek).

H.485/E.495 रीझि आपनी बूझि पर, खीझि विचार–विहीन।
ते उपदेस न मानही, मोह–महादधि–मीन।।

(Who of their wisdom are bewitched,
whose wrath is of confusion born,
In sea of delusions like fish,
good counsel they for ever scorn).

H.488/E.496 निडर ईस तें बीस कै बीसबाहुं सो होइ।
गयो गयो कहें सुमति सब, भयो कुमति कह कोई।।

(Heedless of God if one, indeed,
might of twenty armed king attain,
The wise will name him woe be one,
some fools alone improved acclaim).

H.393/E.518 बड़े बिबुध–दरबार तें भूमि–भूप–दरबार।
जापक पूजक पेखियत, सहत निरादर भार।।

(For sooth greater than courts of gods are
courts of many earthly kings,
For here is seen bearing insult who prays
to God, of His Name sings).

H.534/E.535 आपन छोड़े साथ जब ता दिन हितु न कोइ।
तुलसी अंबुज अंबुबिनुह तासु रिपु होइ।।

(Tulsi, not one remains by side the day one's
own forsaking turns,
When water leaves the lotus bloom,
the sun as foe its petals burns).

H.467/E.542 अनहित भय परहित किए, पर अनहित हितहानि।
तुलसी चारू विचार भल, करिय काज सुनि जानि।।

(Of loss by helping you may fear,
but loss by harming is a fact,
Therefore says Tulsi, it is meet to calmly
think and wisely act).

H.537/E.568 कलि–कुचालि सुभमति–हरनी, सरलै दंडै चक्र।
तुलसी यह निहचय भई, बाढ़ि लेति नब बक्र।।

(Kali Yuga's vice wisdom fair deprives,
'kings punish simple, gentle saints,
Tulsi, for certain this is known:
growing in new forms vice people taints).

H.75/E.99 तुलसी उद्यम करम जग जब जेहि राम सुडीठि।
होइ सुफल सोइ, ताहि सब सनमुख, प्रभु तन पीठि।।

(Says Tulsi, efforts fates bear fruit when
Rama bestows His mercy's grace,
Earthly attachments then are shed and one
beholds Rama's benign face).

H.89/E.223 नाती नाते राम के, रामसनेह सनेहु।
तुलसी माँगत जोरि कर जनम जनम सिव देहु।।

(With folded hands Tulsi begs Thee,
O Shiva grant him this humble prayer,
All bonds for Tulsi be through Rama,
for Rama alone love he may bear).

H.94/E.237 सब साधन को एक फल, जेहि जान्यो सोइ जान।
ज्यों त्यों मन–मंदिर वसहि, राम धरे धनु वान।।

(The wise indeed is one who knows
of all efforts one is aim,
whatever be the means, in heart Rama
with bow arrows may remain).

H.98/E.236 जाने जानत जोइये, बिनु जाने को जान?
तुलसी यह सुनि समुझि हिय आनु धरे धनुवान।।

(Formless knowledge elusive is, few seeking
can ever hope to find,
Says Tulsi, dwel upon this well, Rama with
bow arrow bring in mind).

H.99/E.92 करमठ कठमलिया कहैं, ज्ञानी ज्ञानविहीन।
तुलसी त्रिपथ विहाय गो, रामदुआरे दीन।।

(Karmayogis say: "He wars wood beads;"
He knowledge lacks, learned declare,
In salvation's three paths inept, at Rama's
doorsteps doth Tulsi fare).

H.100/E.98 बाधक सब सब के भए, साधक भए न कोइ।
तुलसी राम कृपालु ते भलो होइ सो होइ।।

(Rough paths of life are full of pits,
support indeed is hard to find,
Tulsi, welfare one gets on earth when gracious
Rama is so inclined).

H.101/E.218 संकरप्रिय मम द्रोही, सिवद्रोही मम दास।
ते नर करहिं कलप भरि घोर नरक महँ वास।।

(Lord said: who love Shiva, oppose Me;
or regard Me but Shiva despise,
Such mortals for a full Kalpa shall in Hell's
eternal fire reside).

H.105/E.97 राम निकाई रावरी है सब ही की नीक।
जो यह साँची है सदा तो नीको तुलसीक।।

(O Rama ! the pleasure of Thy will spells
Welfare for all born on earth,

If this be true, This is sure, of welfare
he shall have no dearth).

H.106/E.100 तुलसी राम जो आदरयो, खोटा खरा खरोइ।
दीपक काजर सिर धरयो, धरयो सु धरयो धरोइ।।

(Tulsi, to whom Rama Mercy gives, worthy or
not, into worth turns,
Lamp holds black soot over its flame
forming collyrium as it burns).

H.107/E.170 तनु विचित्र, कायर बचन, अहि अहार, मन घोर।
तुलसी हरि भए पच्छधर, ताते कह सब मोर।।

(Of unique body, lazy speech, on snakes
hard hearted peacocks dive,
Lord sports their feathers midst his curls
Tulsi, no mortals call them 'Mine').

H.116/E.217 सुद्ध सच्चदानंदमय कदं भानु–कुलकेतु।
चरित करत नर अनुरहत संसृति–सागर–सेतु।।

(O Pure ! O Truth ! Consciousness ! Bliss !
Banner of Surya's clan ! Gracious Rama !
Thy Deeds for mortals are like bridge
to make over Life's sea crossing calm).

H.122/E.115 बालक कोसलपाल के सेवकपाल कृपाल।
तुलसी मन–मानस बसत मंगल मंजु मराल।।

(Child Ram, sweet son of Kaushal's lord,
to save devotees Mercy takes,
Such Rama abides in Tulsi's heart,
like graceful swan sporting in lake).

H.129/E.156 श्रीरघुवीर प्रताप तें सिधु तरे पाषान।
ते मतिमंद जे राम तजि भजहिं जाय प्रभु आन।।

(By Mercy of the Gracious Rama,
rocks floated on waters of seas,
Foolish indeed is one who turns from
such a lord and others seeks).

H.138/E.240 रामचन्द्र के भजन बिनुह जो यह पद निबनि।
झानवंत अपि सोइ नर पसु बिनु पुँछ विरवान।।

(Those who bliss of salvation seek yet
Songs of Rama to sing they fail,
Inspite of learning helpless are like
beasts who lose their horns or tail).

H.149/E.105 तुलसी जाने सुनि समुझि कृपसिन्धु रघुराज।
मंहगे मनि कंचन किए, सौंधे जग, जल नाज।।

(Tulsi has heard and mused in hearts,
Rama is Mercy's ocean he knows,
For gems and gold he costly makes,
but grain and water freely flows).

H.152/E.136 सूधे मन, सूधे वचन, सूधी सब करतूति।
तुलसी सूधी सकल विधि रघुवर–प्रेम–प्रसूति।।

(Whose heart is simple, speech is sweet,
whose actions are gentle and kind,
Tulsi, all ways Rama's love to get such
virtuous ones with ease will find).

H.177/E.233 काल करम गुन दोष जग जीव तिहारे हाथ।
तुलसी रघुवर रावरो, जान जानकीनाथ।।

(In Thy Hand rests all action time qualities
faults, life and its fate,
O Sita's Lord ! Tulsi is Thine ! accept
him and Thine own him make).

H.181/E.157 होहुँ कहावत, सब कहत, राम सहत उपवास।
साहब सीतानाथ से, सेवक तुलसीदास।।

(Tulsi is Rama's devotee called,
to so presume Tulsi too, dares,
Even Sita's Lord with mercy moved
this jest with patient humour bears).

H.273/E.234 कहत कठिन, समुझत कठिन, साधत कठिन विवेक।
होइ घनाक्षरन्याय जौ, पुनि प्रत्यूह अनेक।।

(Terse to expound and to imbibe,
hard is the path knowledge doth preach,
And if perchance it is attained,
obstacles lie ere goal we reach).

H.329/E.429 सदा न जे सुमिरत रहहिं, मिलि न कहहिं प्रियबैन।
तेपै छतिन्हके जाहिं घर जिनके हिय न नैन।।

(Memories in whom do not abide,
who does not with kind words receive,
To him goes only such a one who call of
love cannot perceive).

H.368/E.351 होइ भले के अनभला, होइ दानि के सूम।
होइ कुपूत सुपूत के, ज्यों पावक में धूम।।

(As smoke arises from pure fire,
so evil may from virtue grow,
To generous may be thrifty born
wayward son wealth of worthy throw).

H.371/E.433 जो जो जेहि जेहि रस मगन तहँ सो मुदित मन मानि।
रस गुन दोष विचारिवो रसिकरीति पाहचानि।।

(Of longings which are dear to heart,
in their fulfilment joy one finds,
But of their qualities being aware are
signs of wrapt discerning minds).

H.371/E.435 सम प्रकास–तम पाख दुहूँ नाम भेद विधि कीन्ह।
ससि पोषक सोषक समझि जग जस अपजस दीन्ह।।

(Alike are both halves of the moon,
same are its dark and moon lit nights,
Moon's waxing half bright honour begins,
it waning half moon's repute slights).

H.377/E.489 नीच निरावहिं निरस तरु, तुलसी सीचंहि ऊख।
पोषत पयद समान सब बिष पियूष के रुख।।

(While selfish mortals pullout weeds and
nurture sprouts of sugarcane,
The clouds give every shrub on earth
an equal measure of their rain).

H.393/E.518 बड़े बिबुध–दरबार तें भूमि–भप दरबार।
जापक पूजक पेखियत, सहत निरादर भार।।

(For sooth greater than courts of gods are
courts of many earthly kings,
For here is seen bearing insult who
prays to God, of His Name sings).

H.408/E.328 बचन वेष क्यों जानिए मन मलीन नर नारि।
सूपनखा, मृग, पूतना, दसमुख, प्रमुख विचारि।।

(From outward show of speech and form
can one low hearts of mortal find?
Bring Ravana, Maricha Surpanakha and
Putna's conduct to your mind).

H.447/E.410 तुलसी असमय के सखा, धीरज, धर्म, विवेक।
साहित, साहस, सत्यव्रत, रामभरोसो एक।।

(Tulsi in distress these are friends,
patience, discernment, book of dharma,
Courage, unswerving path of Truth,
towards Rama to look stand fast and firm).

H.467/E.542 अनहित भय परहित किए, पर–अनहित हितहानि।
तुलसी चारु विचार भल, करिय काज सुनि जानि।।

(Of loss by helping you may fear,
but loss by harming is a fact,
Therefore, says Tulsi, it is meet to
calmly think and wisely act).

H.481/E.408 तुलसी स्वारथ सामुहो, परमारथ तनु पीठि।
अंध कहै दुख पाइहो, डिठियारो केहि डीठि।।

(Tulsi, who looks to selfish ends and
turning from salvation flies,
To be called sightless hurts his heart
but how can one say he has eyes?)

H.486/E.421 अनसमुझे अनुसोचनो, अवसि अवसि समुझिए आपु।
तुलसी आपु न समझिए पलपल पर परितापु।।

(What you cannot first understand,
reflect and it will then be known,

What you cannot be yourself grasp,
to grief each moment will be prone).

H.489/E.341 जो सुनि समुझि अनीतिरतु जागत रहे जु सोई।
उपदेसिवो जगाइवो तुलसी उचित न होइ।।

(Who grasp all things of them aware yet
heart in ways of vice has lain,
He seems awake, yet in asleep, to wake him,
Tulsi is in vain).

H.490/E.493 बहु मुख, बहु रूचि, बहु बचन, बहु आचार व्यवहार।
इनको भलो मनाइवो, यह अज्ञान अपार।।

(Too many children who desires,
lazy whose ways, action and speech,
Dome fortune such mortals eludes,
in folly they their welfare seek).

H.495/E.434 तुलसी भेड़ी की धँसनि जड़–जनता–सनमान।
उपजत ही अभिमान भी, खोवत मूढ़ अपान।।

(Support of rustic masses weak is like
that of a herd of sheep,
Foolish turn proud when thus acclaimed,
their minds discernment do not keep).

H.496/E.463 लही आँख कब आँधरे, बाँझ पूत कब ल्याय?
कब कोढ़ी काया लही? जग बहराइच जाइ।।

(To Bahraich all in fervour rush,
but who to ask himself has paused;
Has one gained sight, been blest with child,
or leper's skin has healing caused?)

H.537/E.558 कलि–कुचालि सुममति–हरिन, सरलै दंडै चक्र।
तुलसी यह निहचय भई, बाढ़ि लेति नव बक्र।।

(Kali Yuga's vice wisdom fair deprives,
kings punish simple, gentle saints,
Tulsi, for certain this is known ;
growing in new form vice people taints).

8

Selection from Ramcharitmanas (Balakanda)

श्रीरामायण जी की आरती

आरती श्रीरामायनजी की। कीरति कलित ललित सिय पी की।।
गावत ब्रह्मादि मुनि नारद। बालमीक बिग्यान बिसारद।।
सुक सनकादि सेष अरु सारद। बरनि पवनसुत कीरति नीकी।।
गावत वेद पुरान अष्टदस। छओ सास्त्र सब ग्रंथन को रस।।
मुनि जन धन संतन को सरबस। सार अंस संमत सबही की।।
गावत संतत संभु भवानी। अरु घटसंभव मुनि बिग्यानी।।
ब्यास आदि कविबज बखानी। कागभुसुंडि गरुड़ के ही की।।
कलि मल हरनि बिषय रस फिकी। सुभग सिंगार मुक्ति जुबती की।।
दलन रोग भव मूरि अमी की। तात मात सब बिधि तुलसी की।।

An Arati Song

(A hymn of praise addressed to Shri Ramayana at the time of waving lights while worshipping the same)
(Render into English verse by Madhava Sarana, M.A., L.L.B.)
Soft lights we wave, soft lights display, The wealth of sages; yet what not
Before this Lord of Sita's lay-off all the saints ? their mainstay,
The Ramayana, so sweet and dear, Uma and Sankara e'er intone,
So beautiful, without a peer, As well the wise Agastya pot grown,
Which god like Brahma, Narada sing, The crows, Garud's it heart indwell,
The ant-hill sage, soul seers king. The poets great like Vyasa and else,
Suka, Sarada, Sesa, boy sages four, In ecstasies this song relay.
The wind-gods' son recount this lore – Shuns sensuous joy, sin's abluent,

With great delight and voices gay. The dome of Muktis ornament,
The holy books their music mix, Ambrosial herb rebirth to cure,
To sing this gist of Sastras six, And parents both, its only sure
of all good works, of all good thought; For Tulsidas in everywhere.

जथा सुअंजन अंजि हग साधक सिद्ध सुजान।
कौतुक देखत सैल बन भूतल भूरि निधान।।१।।

(— as for instance, by applying to the eyes the miraculous salve known by the name of Siddhanjana (the eye salve of perfection) strives, adepts as well as men of wisdom easily discover a host of mines on hill tops, in the midst of forests and in the bowels of the earth).[1]

सुनि समुझहिं जन मुदित मन मज्जहिं अति अनुराग।
लहहिं चारि फल अछत तनु साधु समाज प्रयाग।।२।।

(Men who having heard the glory of this moving Prayaga in the form of the assemblages of holy men appreciate it with an enraptured mind and then take a plunge into it with extreme devotion obtain the four rewards of human existence during their very lifetime.[2]

बंदऊँ संत समान चित हित अनहित नहिं कोइ।
अंजलि गत सुभ सुमन जिपि सम सुगंध कर दोइ।।३ क।।

संत सरत चित जगत हित जानि सुभाउ सनेहु।
बाल–विनय सुनि करि कृपा राम चरन रति देहु।।३ ख।।

(I bow to the saints, who are even minded towards all and have no friend or foe, just as a flower of good quality placed in the palm of one's hands communicates its fragrance alike to both the hands (the one which plucked it and that which held and preserved it). Realizing thus the noble disposition and loving nature of saints, who are innocent at heart and catholic in spirit. I make this humble submission to them. Listening to my childlike prayer and taking compassion on me. O noble souls, bless me with devotion to the feet of Shri Rama)

उदासीन अरि मीत हित सुनत जरहिं खल रीति।
जानि पानि जुग जोरि जन बिनती करइ सप्रीति।।४।।

(The wicked burn with jealousy as they hear of other's welfare, be they his friends, foes or neutrals: Such is their wont. Knowing thus this humble soul makes loving entreaties to them with joined palms).

भलो भलाइहि पै लहइ लहइ निचाइहि नीचु।
सुधा सराहिअ अमरताँ गरल सराहिआ मीचु।।५।।

(Of course, a good man has a bias for goodness alone, while a vile person is prone to vileness. While nectar is praised for its immortalizing virtue, position is extolled for its deadly effects).

जड़ चेतन गुन दोषमय बिस्व कीन्ह करतार।
संत हंस गुन गहहिं पच परिहरि वारि विकार।।६।।

(God has created the universe consisting of animate and inanimate beings as partaking of both good and evil; swans in the form of saints imbibe the milk of goodness rejecting water in the form of evil).

ग्रह भेषज जल पवन पर पाइ कुजोग सुजोग।
होहिं कुबस्तु सुबस्तु जग लखहिं सुलच्छन लोग।।७ क।।

सम प्रकास तप पाख दुहुँ नाम भेद विधि कीन्ह।
ससि सोषक पोषक समुझि जग जस अपजस दीन्ह।।७ ख।।

जड़ चेतन जग जीव जतसकल राममय जानि।
बदऊँ सब के पद कमल सदा जोरि जुगपानि।।७ ग।।

देव दनुज नर नाग खग प्रेत पितर गंधर्व।
बंदउँ किंनर रजनिचर कृपा करहु अब सर्व।।७ घ।।

The planets, medicines, water, air and cloth prove good or bad in the world according to their good or evil associations; only men endowned with a keen insight are able to know this. The proportion of moonlight and darkness is the same in the bright as well as in the dark fortnight; only the two have been named differently by the creator. Knowing the one as the nourisher and the other as the emaciator of the moon, the world has given it a good name and a bad one. Whatever beings, animate or inanimate, there are in the universe, recognizing them, one and all as consisting of Shri Rama. I ever adore the lotus feet of all with joined palms. I reverence gods, demons, human beings, Nagas, birds, spirits, manes (the souls of departed ancestors) and Gandharvas, Kinnaras and Raksasas (giants). Pray be gracious to me all on this occasion.

भाग छोर अभिलाषु बड़ करउँ एक विस्वास।
पैहहिं सुख सुनि सुजन सब खल करिहहिं उपहास।।८।।

(Humble is my lot and my ambition high; my only hope is that all good men will be gratified to hear what I say, while the evil minded will laugh).

भनिति मोरि सब गुन रहित बिस्व बिदित गुन एक।
सो विचारि सुनिहहिं सुमति जिन्ह के बिमल बिवेक।।६।।

(My composition is devoid of all charm; it has only one merit, which is known throughout the world. Recognizing this merit, men of sound reason, who are gifted with unbiased judgement, will surely hear it).

प्रिय लागहि अति सबहि मम भनिति राम जग संग।
दारु बिचारु कि करइ काउ बंदिआ मलय प्रसंग।।१० क।।
स्याम सुरभि पय बिसद अति गुनद करहिं सब पान।
गिरा ग्राम्य सिय राम जस गावहिं सुनहिं सुजान।।१० ख।।

(My composition will appear extremely delightful to all by its association with the glory of Shri Rama, even as timber of every description is transformed into sandal and becomes worthy of adoration by contact with the Malaya mountain (in South India), and nobody takes into account the quality of wood in that region. The milk of even a dark cow is white and possesses a great medicinal value and is drunk by all. So do the wise chunt and hear the glory of Sita and Rama even though couched in the vulgar tongue.

जुगुति बेधि पुनि पोहिअहिं रामचरित बर ताग।
पहिरहिं सज्जन बिमल उर सोभा अति अनुराग।।११।।

(If those pearls are pierced with skill and strung together on the beautiful thread of Shri Rama's exploits, and if noble souls wear them in their innocent heart, grace in the form of excessive foundless is the result).

सारद सेस महेस विधि आगम निगम पुरान।
नेति नेति कहि जासु गुन करहिं निरंतर गान।।१२।।

(Goddess Sarasvati, Sesa (the thousand headed serpent god), the great Lord Siva, Brahma (the creator), the Agamas (Tantras), the Vedas and the Puranas unceasingly sing His virtues, saying 'not that' 'not that').

अति अपार जे सरित बर जौं नृप सेतु कराहिं।
चढ़ि पिपीलिकउ परम लघु बिनु श्रम पारहि जाहिं।।१३।।

(If kings get bridges constructed over big rivers, which are too broad, even the tiniest ants cross them without exertion).

सरल कबित कीरति बिमल सोइ आदरहिं सुजान।
सहज बयर बिसराइ रिपु जो सुनि करहिं बखान।।१४ क।।

सो न होइ बिनु बिमल मति मोहि मति बल अति थोर।
करहु कृपा हरि जस कहऊँ पुनि पुनि करउँ निहोर।।१४ ख।।

कवि कोविद रघुवर चरित मानस मंजु मराल।
बाल विनय सुनि सुरुचि लखि मोपर होहु कृपाल।।१४ ग।।

(The wise admire only that poetry which is lucid and portrays a spotless character and which even opponents hear with applause forgetting natural animosity. Such poetry is not possible without a refined intellect and of intellectual power I have very little. Be gracious, therefore so that I may depict the glory of Sri Hari, I solicit again and again. Poets and wise men, lovely swans sporting in the Mansarovara lake of Shri Rama's exploits ! hearing my childlike prayer and recognizing my refined taste).

सपनेहुँ साचेहुँ मोहि पर जौं हर गौरि पसाउ।
तौ फुर होउ जो कहेउँ सब भाषा भनिति प्रभाउ।।१५।।

(If Hari and Gauri (Lord Shiva and Parvati) are really propitious to me, even in dream, let all that I have said in glorification of this poetry of mine, written in a popular dialect, come out true).

बंदउँ अवध भुआल सत्य प्रेम जेहि राम पद।
बिछुरत दीनदयाल प्रिय तनु तून इव परिहरेउ।।१६।।

(I adore the king of Ayodhya, who cherished such true love for the feet of Shri Rama that he gave up his clear life as a mere straw the moment the Lord, who is compassionate to the poor parted from him).

प्रनवउँ पवनकुमार खल बन पावक ग्यानधन।
जासु हृदय आगार बसहिं राम सर चाप धर।।१७।।

(I greet Hanuman, the son of the wind-god, an embodiment of wisdom, who is fire as it were for the forest of the wicked, and in the abode of whose heart resides Shri Rama equipped with a bow and arrows).

गिरा अरथ जल बीचि सम कहिअत भिन्न न भिन्न।
बंदउँ सीता राम पद जिन्हहि परम प्रिय खिन्न।।१८।।

(I reverence the feet of Sita and Rama, who though stated to be different and yet identical just like a word and its meaning or like water and the waves on its surface, and to whom the afflicted are most dear).

बरषा रितु रघुपति भगति तुलसी सालि सुदास।
राम नाम बर बरन जुग सावन भादव मास।।१६।।

(Devotion to the Lord of Raghus is, as it were, the rainy season and the noble devotees, says Tulsidas, represent the paddy crop; while the two charming syllables of the name 'Rama' stand for the two months of Sravana and Bhadrapada (corresponding roughly to July and August).

एकु छत्रु एकु मुकुटमनि सब बरननि पर जोउ।
तुलसी रघुवर नाम के बरन विराजत दोउ।।२०।।

(Lo ! the two letters (रा and म) forming part of the name of Raghuvara (the Chief of the Raghu) crown all the letters of the Alphabet, the one spreading like an umbrella and the other resting as a crest jewel. O Tulsidas).

राम नाम मनिदीप धरू जीह दहरी द्वार।
तुलसी भीतर बाहेरहुँ जौं चाहसि उजिआर।।२१।।

(Instal the luminous gem in the shape of the divine name 'Rama' on the threshold of the tongue at the doorway of your mouth, if you will have light both inside and outside. O Tulsidasa).

सकल कामना हीन जे राम भगति रस लीन।
नाम सुप्रेम पियूष ह्रद तिन्हहुँ किए मन मीन।।२२।।

(Even those who are free from all desires and absorbed in the joy of devotion to Shri Rama have thrown their heart as fish into the nectarine lake of supreme affection for the Name).

निरगुन तें एहि भांति बड़ नाम प्रभाउ अपार।
कहउँ नामु बड़ राम तें निज विचार अनुसार।।२३।।

(The glory of the Name is thus infinitely greater than that of the Absolute: I shall show below how in my judgement the Name is superior even to Shri Ram).

सबरी गीध सुसेवकनि सुगति दीन्हि रघुनाथ।
नाम उधारे अमित खल वेद विदित गुन गाथ।।२४।।

(The Lord of Raghus conferred immortality only on faithful servants like Sabari (the celebrated Bhila women) and the vulture (Jatayu) while His name has delivered innumerable wretches; the tale of its virtues is well-known in the Vedas).

ब्रह्म राम तें नामु बड़ बर दायक बर दानि।
रामचरित सत कोटि महँ लिय महेस जियँ जानि।।२५।।

(The Name is thus greater than Brahma and Shri Rama both and confers blessings even on the bestowers of boons. Knowing this in His heart, the great Lord Siva chose this word (Rama) for Himself out of Shri Rama's story comprising 100 crore verses. The Ramayana as originally composed by Brahma himself and delivered to Lord Shiva through Narada is believed to have contained as many as a 100 crore verses).

नामु राम को कलपतरू कलि कल्यान निवासु।
जो सुमिरत भयो भाँग तें तुलसी तुलसीदासु।।२६।।

(The name of Rama is a wish yielding tree, the very home of beutitude in this age of Kali, by remembering which Tulsidas (the poet himself) was transformed from an intoxicating drug like the hemp-plant into the holy basil).

राम नाम नर केसरी कनककसिपु कलिकाल।
जापक जन प्रहलाद जिमि पालिहि दलि सुरसाल।।२७।।

(To use another metaphor) the Name of Rama is, as it were, the Lord manifested as a Man lion and the age of Kali, the demon Hiranyakasipu. Crushing this enemy of gods, the Name will protect the devotees repeating it, even as the Man-lion protected Prahalad).

सठ सेवक की प्रीति रूचि रखिहहिं राम कृपालु।
उपल किए जलजान जेहि सचिव सुमति कपि भालु।।२८ क।।

हौहुं कहावत सबु कहत राम सहत उपहास।
साहिब सीतानाथ सो सेवक तुलसीदास।।२८ ख।।

(The benevolent Rama will nonetheless respect the devotion and pleasure of this wicked servant -— Shri Rama, who made barks out of rocks and wise counsellors out of monkeys and bears. Everybody calls me a servant of the Lord and I myself claim to be one; and Shri Rama puts up with the sceoffing remark that a master like Sita's Lord has a servant like Tulsidas).

प्रभु तरू तर कपि डार पर ते किए आपु समान।
तुलसी कहुँ न राम से साहिब सीलनि धान।।२६ क।।

राम निकाइ राबरी है सबही को नीक।
जौं सह सांची है सदा तौ नीको तुलसीक।।२६ ख।।

एहि विधि निज गुन दोष कहि सबहि बहुरि सिरू नाइ।
बरनउँ रघुवर विसद जसु सुनि कलि कलुष नसाइ।। २६ ग।।

(While the Lord sat at the foot of trees, the monkeys perched themselves high on the boughs; such creatures He exalted to his own position ! There is no Lord so generous as Shri Rama, O Tulsidas ! your goodness, O Rama, is beneficient to all; if this is a fact, Tulsidas too will be blessed by the same. Thus revealing my merits and demerits and bowing my head once more to all, I proceed to sing the immaculate glory of the chief of Raghus, by hearing which the impurities of the Kali age are wiped away).

मैं पुनि निज गुरू सन सुनी कथा सो सूकरखेत।
समुझी नहीं तसि बालपन तब अति रहेउँ अचेत।।३० क।।

श्रोता बकता ग्याननिधि कथा राम कै गूढ़।
किमि समुझौं मैं जीव जड़ कलि मल प्रसित विमूढ़।।३० ख।।

(Then I heard the same story in the holy Sukaraksetra* (the modern Soron in the Western United Provinces) from my preciptor; but as I had no sense in those days of my childhood. I could not follow it full well. Both the listener and the reciter of the mysterious story of Shri Rama must be repositories of wisdom.How, then could I a dull and stupid creature steeped in the impurities of the kali age, expect to follow it.

राम कथा मंदाकिनी चित्रकूट चित चारू।
तुलसी सुभग सनेह बन सिय रघुवीर बिहारु।।३१।।

(The story of Shri Rama is the river Mandakini (which washes the foot of Chitrakuta), a guileless heart is Mount Chitrakuta (one of the happy resorts of Shri Rama during his wanderings in the forest) while pure love, says Tulsidasa, is the woodland in which Sita and Rama carry on their divine pastimes.

---

*The name is associated with the descent of Shri Hari as a Boar (Sukara) who killed Hiranyakspa, the elder brother of Hiranyakasipu and lifted up the earth from the depths of the ocean, to which it had been consigned by the said demon.

कुपथ कुतरक कुचालि कलि कपट दंभ पाषंड।
दहन राम गुन ग्राम जिमि इधंन अनल प्रचंड।।३२क।।

रामचरित राकेस कर सरिस सुखद सब काहु।
सज्जन कुमुद चकोर चित हित बिसेषि बड़ लाहु।।३२ख।।

(The hosts of virtues possessed by Shri Rama are like a blazing fire to consume the dry wood of evil ways, fallacious reasoning, mischievous practices, deceit, hypocrisy and hersey prevailing in Kali. The exploits of Shri Rama are delightful to one and all even as the rays of the full moon; they are particularly agreeable and highly beneficial to the mind of the virtuous, who can be compared to the white water lily and the Chkora bird.

राम अनंत अनंत गुन अमित कथा विस्तार।
सुनि आचरजु न मानिहहिं जिन्ह के बिमल विचार।।३३।।

(Rama is infinite, infinite are His virtues and the dimensions of His story are also immeasurable. Those whose thoughts are pure will, therefore, feel no surprise when they hear it).

मज्जहिं सज्जन बृंद बहु पावन सरजु नीर।
जपहिं राम धारि ध्यान उर सुन्दर स्याम सरीर।।३४।।

(Numerous groups of pious men take dip in the holy water of the Sarayu river and visualizing in their heart the beautiful swarthy form of Shri Rama, mutter His name).

जस मानस जेहि विधि भयउ जग प्रचार जेहि हेतु।
अब सोइ कहउँ प्रसंग सब सुमिरि उमा वृषकेतु।।३५।।

(Invoking Uma (Goddess Parvati) and Lord Siva (who has a bull emblazoned on His standard), I now proceed to give a full account as to what this Ramcharitmanas is like, how it came to be and what led to its popularity in the world).

सुठि सुंदर संवाद बर विरचे बुद्धि विचारि।
तेह एहि पावन सुभग सर घाट मनोहर चारि।।३६।।

(The four most beautiful and excellent dialogues (viz., those between (i) Bhusandi and Garuda, (ii) Siva and Parvati (iii) Yajnavalkya and Bharadvaja and (iv) between Tulsidas and other saints) that have been cleverly woven into this narrative are the four lovely Ghatas of this holy and charming lake).

पुलक बाटिका वाग बन सुख सुविहंग विहारू।
माली सुमन सनेह जल सींचत लोचन चारू।।३७।।

(The thrill of joy that one experiences while listening to this narrative represents the flower gardens, orchards and groves, and the delight one feels is the sporting of birds while a noble mind is the gardner, who waters the garden etc. with the moisture of love through the charming jars of eyes).

जे श्रद्धा संबल रहित नहिं संतन्ह कर साथ।
तिन्ह कहुँ मानस अगम अति जिन्हहि न प्रिय रघुनाथ।।३८।।

(The Manasa is most inaccessible to those who lack provisions for the journey in the shape of piety who do not enjoy the company of saints and who have no love for the Lord of Raghus Shri Rama).

श्रोता त्रिविध समाजपुर ग्राम नगर दुहुँ कूल।
संतसभा अनुपम अवध सकल सुमंगल मूल।।३९।।

(The three type of audience are the towns, villages and cities on both the banks; and the congregation of saints in the incomparable Ayodhya, which is the fountain of all auspicious blessings).

बालचरित चहु बंधु के बनज विपुल बहुरंग।
नृप रानी परिजन सुकृत मधुकर वारिविहंग।।४०।।

(The childlike sports of the four divine brothers are the numerous lotus flowers of varied colours; while the stock of merits of King Dasaratha and his consorts and court represent the bees and water birds).

समन अमित उतपात सब भरत चरित जपजाग।
कलि अध खल अक्गुन कथन ते जलमल बग काग।।४१।।

(The story ofBharata, which wards off all calamities, is a congregational muttering of sacred for mulae carried on at the river bank; while the references to the corruptions of the Kali age and to the evil propensities of wicked souls represent the scum on the water as well as the herons and crows living by the riverside).

अवलोकनि बोलनि मिलनि प्रीति परसपर हास।
भायम भलि यहु बंधु की जल माधुरी सुवास।।४२।।

(The way the four brothers look at one another, talk with one another meet and love one another, their mirth and their ideal brotherliness these constitute the sweetness and fragrance of the water).

मति अनुहारि सुवारि गुन गन गनि मन अन्हवाइ।
सुमिरि भषानी संकरहि कह कवि कथा सुहाइ।।४३क।।
अब रघुपति पद पंकरूह हियँ धरि पाइ प्रसाद।
कहउँ जुगल मुनिबर्य कर मिलन सुभग संवाद।।४३ख।।

(Having enumerated the virtues of this excellent water to the best of his intellectual capacity and bathed his mind in it, and remembering Goddess Bhavani (Parvati) and Lord Sankara, the poet (Tulsidas) narrates the beautiful story. Installing in my heart the lotus feet of the Lord of Raghus and thus securing His grace, I now proceed to relate the charming story of the meeting of the two great sages (Yajnavalkya and Bharadvaja).

ब्रह्म निरूपन धरम विधि वरनहिं तत्व विभाग।
कहहिं भगति भगवंत कैं संजुत ग्यान विराग।।४४।।

(They discuss the nature of Brahma (the Supreme Eternal), the precepts of religion and the classification of fundamental entities and expatiate on Devotion to the Lord coupled with spiritual enlightenment and dispassion).

संत कहहिं असि नीति प्रभु श्रुति पुरान मुनि गात।
होइ न विमल विवेक उर गुर सन किएँ दुराव।।४५।।

(The saints lay down the rule, and the Vedas as well as the Puranas and sages too loudly proclaim, that pure wisdom cannot dawn in the heart, should one keep anything concealed from one's spiritual preceptor).

प्रभु सोइ राम कि अपर कोउ जाहि जपत त्रिपुरारि।
सत्यधाम सर्वग्य तुम्ह कहहु विवेकु विचारि।।४६।।

(Is it this very, Rama, my lord, or some one else whose name the slayer of the demon Tripura, Siva, ever repeats? You are an embodiment of truth and omniscient; so ponder well and give me your considered reply).

कहउँ सो मति अनुहारि अब उमा संभु संवाद।
भयउ समय जेहि हेतु जेहि सुनु मुनि मिटिहि विषाद।।४७।।

(I shall repeat now to the best of my lights the dialogue between

Uma (Goddess Parvati) and Sambhu (Lord Siva). Here, O sage, the time and the occasion of this dialogue; your gloom will be lifted).

हृदयँ बिचारत जात हर केहि बिधि दरसनु होइ।
गुप्त रुप अवतरेउ प्रभु गाएँ जान सबु कोइ।।४८क।।

संकट उर अति छोभु सती न जानहिं मरमु सोइ।
तुलसी दरसन लोभु मन डरू लोचन लालची।।४८ख।।

(Lord Hara (Siva) kept pondering as he went. "How can I obtain a sight of Him? The Lord has bodied Himself forth secretly; and if I visit Him, everyone will know who He is". In Sankara's heart there was a great tumult; Sati, however had no inkling of this secret. His mind, says Tulsidas, apprehended lest the secret might be disclosed while the temptation of obtaining a sight of the Lord made His eyes wistful).

अति विचित्र रघुपति चरित जानहिं परम सुजान।
जे मतिमंद विमोह बस हृदयं धरहि कछु आन।।४६।।

(Exceedingly mysterious are the ways of the Lord of Raghus; the supremely wise alone can comprehend them. The dull witted in their height of folly imagine something quite different).

ब्रह्मा जो ब्यापक बिरज अज अकल अनीह अभेद।
सो कि देह धरि होड़ नर जाहि न जानत वेद।।५०।।

(The Supreme Eternal, which is all pervading, unbegotten without parts, free from desire, beyond Maya and beyond all distinction and which not even the Vedas can comprehend can it assume the shape of a man)?".

लाग न उर उपदेसु जदपि कहेउ सिवँ बार बहु।
बोले बिहसि महेसु हरि माया बलु जानि जियँ।।५१।।

(Although Lord Siva repeated this time after time, His exhortation made no impression on the heart of Sati. Then the great Lord Siva smilingly said, realizing in His heart the potency of Shri Haris Maya:

पुनि पुनि हृदयँ विचारू करि धरि सीता कर रूप।
आगें होइ चलि पंथ तेहिं जेहि आवत नर भूप।।५२।।

(After many an anxious thought Sati assume the form of Sita and moved ahead on the same route along which the Ruler of men (Shri Rama) was passing).

राम बचन मृदु गूढ़ सुनि उपजा अति संकोचु।
सती सभीत महेस पहिं चलीं हृदयँ बड़ सोचु।।५३।।

(Sati felt very uncomfortable when she heard these soft yet significant words of Rama. She turned towards the great Lord Siva with a feeling of awe and much dejected at heart).

सती बिधात्री इंदिरा देखी अमित अनूप।
जेहिं जेहिं बेष अजादि सुर तेहि तेहि तन अनुरूप।।५४।।

(She further perceived innumerable Satis (consorts of Siva), consorts of Brahma and Laksmis (consorts of Vishnu), all peerless in beauty. They conformed in their appearance to the garb in which Brahma and the other gods appeared).

गई समीप महेस तब हंसि पूछी कुसलात।
लीन्हि परीछा कवन बिधि कहहु सत्य सब बात।।५५।।

(When she came near, Lord Siva smilingly inquired if all was well with Her and then said, "Tell me now the whole truth, how did you test Shri Rama?).

परम पुनीत न जाइ तजि किएँ प्रेम बड़ पापु।
प्रगटि न कहत महेसु कछु हृदयँ अधिक संतापु।।५६।।

(Sati is too chaste to be abandoned, and it is a great sin to love her any more as a wife. The great Lord Siva uttered not a word aloud, although there was great agony in His heart).

सतीं हृदयँ अनुमान किय सबु जानेउ सर्वग्य।
कीन्ह कपटु मैं संभु सन नारि सहज जड़ अग्य।।५७क।।

(Sati concluded that the omniscient Lord had come to know everything and felt sorry that she had tried to deceive Sambhu. The women is silly and stupid by nature, she realized).

जलु पय सरिस बिकाइ देखहु प्रीति कि रीति भलि।
बिलग होइ रसु जाइ कपट खटाई परत पुनि।।५७ख।।

(Even water (when mixed with milk) sells as milk; look at the unifying process of love. The water, however, is separated from the milk and the taste also disappears the moment a drop of acid is introduced into it in the form of a falsehood).

सती बसहि कैलास तब अधिक सोचु मन माहिं।
मामु न कोऊ जान कछु जुग सम दिवस सिराहि।।५८।।

(Then Sati dwelt in Kailasa, Her mind grievously sorrowing. No body knew anything about what was going on in Her mind; but the days hung heavy on Her like so many Yugas or ages).

तौ सबदरसी सुनिअ प्रभु करउ सो बेगि उपाइ।
होइ मरनु जेहिं बिनहिं श्रम दुसह बिपति बिहाइ।।५६।।

("Then O all perceiving Lord, listen to me and speedily devise some plan whereby I may die and be thus rid of this unbearable calamity without much exertion).

दच्छ लिए मुनि बोलि सब करन लगे बड़ जाग।
नेवते सादर सकल सुर जे पावत मख भाग।।६०।।

(Daksa got together all the sages and they began to perform a big sacrifice. All the gods who obtain a share of the oblations offered at a sacrifice were cordially invited to attend).

पिता भवन उत्सव परम जौं प्रभु आपसु होइ।
तौ मैं जाउँ कृपायतन सादर देखन सोइ।।६१।।

(There is great rejoicing at my father's house, O Lord, If you grant me leave, I would faingo and see it. O storehouse of compassion).

कहि देखा हर जतन बहु रहइ न दच्छकुमारि।
दिए मुख्य गन संग तब बिदा कीन्ह त्रिपुरारि।।६२।।

(Having reasoned with Her in ways more than one when Hara at last perceived that the daughter of Daksa was not going to stay, the slayer of Tripura detailed a few of His principal attendants as Her escort and sent Her away).

सिब अपमानु न जाइ सहि हृदयँ न होइ प्रबोध।
सकल समहि हठि हटकि तब बोलीं बचन सक्रोध।।६३।।

(The insult to Siva was something unbearable; Her heart could not, therefore, be pacified. Then, sharply reproaching the whole assembly, she spoke in angry accents).

सती मरनु सुनि संभु गन लगे करन मख खीस।
जग्य बिधंस बिलोकि भृगु रच्छा कीन्हि मुनीस।।६४।।

(Hearing of Sati's death, the attendants of Sambhu began to destroy the sacrifice. Seeing the sacrifice being destroyed, the great sage Bhrgu protected it).

सदा सुमन फल रहित सब द्रुम नव नाना जाति।
प्रगटीं सुन्दर सैल पर मनि आकर बहु भाँति।।६५।।

(Young trees of different varieties were endowned with never failing blossoms and fruits, and mines of jewels of various kinds appeared on the beautiful mountain).

त्रिकालग्य सर्वग्य तुम्ह गति सर्वत्र तुम्हारि।
कहहु सुता के दोष गुन मुनिवर हृदयँ विचारि।।६६।।

(You know everything including the past, present and future, and have access everywhere. Therefore, O good sage, tell me what is good and what is bad about my daughter after a mature consideration).

जोगी जटिल अकाम मन नगन अमंगल वेष।
अस स्वामी एहि कहँ मिलिहि परी हस्त असि रेख।।६७।।

(An ascetic with matted hair and a heart devoid of longing, stark naked and with hideous accoutrements-such a one shall be her lord, as I can read from the lives of her palm).

कह मुनीस हिमवंत सुनु जो विधि लिखा लिलार।
देव दनुज नर नाग मुनि कोउ न भटेनिहार।।६८।।

(The chief of sages, Narada, replied: Hear, O Himavan; whatever has been decreed by Fate no one can undo-not even gods, demons, human beings, Nagas or sages).

जौं अस हिसिषा करहिं नर जड़ विवेक अभिमान।
परहिं कलप भरि नरक महुँ जीव कि ईस समान।।६९।।

(If in their pride of wisdom foolishmen emulate the great, they are cast into hell for a whole Kalpa or life time of the universe. Can an embodied soul vie with God)?

अस कहि नारद सुमिरि हरि गिरिजहि दीन्हि असीस।
होइहि यह कल्यान अब संसय तजहु गिरीस।।७०।।

(So saying and with his thoughts fixed on Sri Hari, Narada gave his blessings to Girija and said, "Shell all fear, O Lord of mountains, all will now turn out well).

प्रिया सोजु परिहरहु सबु सुमिरहु श्री भगवान।
पारवतिहि निरमयउ जेहिं सोइ करिहि कल्यान।।७१।।

(Put away all anxiety, my dear, and fix your thoughts on the Lord. He alone who has created Parvati will bring her happiness).

सुनहि मातु मैं दीख अस सपन सुनावउँ तोहि।
सुन्दर गौर सुविप्रबर अस उपदेसेउ मोहि।।७२।।

(Listen mother: I relate to you a vision which I saw. A handsome and fair complexioned noble Brahmana gave me the following exhortation).

बेदसिरा मुनि आइ तब सवहि कहा समुझाइ।
पारवती महिमा सुनत रहे प्रबोधहि पाइ।।७३।।

(The sage Vedasira then came and consoled them all. They were comforted when they heard of the glory of Parvati).

भयउ मनोरथ सुफल तब सुनु गिरिराजकुमारि।
परिहरू दुसह कलेस सब अब मिलिहहिं त्रिपुरारि।।७४।।

(Listen, O daughter of mountain king; your desire is accomplished. Cease all your rigorous penance; the slayer of Tripura will soon be yours).

चिदानंद सुखधाम सिब विगत मोह मद काम।
बिचरहिं महि धरि हृदयँ हरि सकल लोक अभिराम।।७५।।

(The embodiment of intelligence and bliss, the abode of happiness, Siva, who is ever free from error, arrogance and desire, roamed about on earth with His heart fixed on Sri Hari, the delight of the whole world).

अब विनती मम सुनहु सिब जौं मो पर निज नेहु।
जाइ विवाहहु सैलजहि यह मोहि मांगें देहु।।७६।।

(Now, Siva, if you have any affection for Me, listen to My appeal. Go and marry Sailaja (the daughter of Himacala); grant this boon to me).

पारवती पहिं जाइ तुम्ह प्रेम परिच्छा लेहु।
गिरिहि प्रेरि पठएहु भवन दूरि करेहु संदेहु।।७७।।

(Going to Parvati, you put her love to the test. Then directing her father, Himalaya, to her, send her back to her home and dispel her doubts).

सुनत बचन बिहसे रिषय गिरिसंभव तब देह।
नारद कर उपदेसु सुनि कहहु बसउ किसु गेह।।७८।।

(Hearing the above reply the sages laughed and said, "After all your body owes its existence to a mountain (Himalaya); tell us who has ever listened to Narada's advice and lived in his home").

अब सुख सोवत सोचु नहिं भीख मागि भव खाहिं।
सहज एकाकिन्ह के भवन कबहुँ कि नारि खटाहिं।।७९।।

(Siva is care free now; he lives on alms and enjoys a sound sleep. Can women ever stay in the house of habitual recluses)?

महादेव अवगुन भवन बिष्नु सकल गुन धाम।
जेहि कर मनु रस जाहि सन तेहि सन काम।।८०।।

(The great God Siva may be full of faults and Vishnu may be a repository of all virtues. One is, however concerned with him alone who gladdens one's heart).

तुम्ह माया भगवान सिव सकल जगत पितु मातु।
नाइ चरन सिर मुनि चलने पुनि पुनि हरषत गातु।।८१।।

("You are Maya, while Siva is God Himself, you are the parents of the whole universe". Bowing their head at the feet of Parvati, they departed. A thrill ran through their frame again and again).

सब सन कहा बुझाइ विधि दनुज निधन तब होइ।
संभु सुक्र संभूत सुत एहि जीतह रन सोइ।।८२।।

("Brahma reassured them all saying", The demon shall die only when there is a son sprung from the loins of Sambhu for he alone can subdue the demon in battle).

सुरन्ह कही निज विपति सब सुनि मन कीन्ह विचार।
संभु विरोध न कुसल मोहि विहसि कहेउ अस मार।।८३।।

(The god told him all their distress, hearing their tale, the god of love pondered and spoke thus with a smile, "I except no good results for myself hostility to Sambhu").

जे सजीव जग अचन चर नारि पुरूष अस नाम।
ते निज निज मरजाद तजि भए सकल बस काम।।८४।।

(Whatever creature existed in the world, whether animate or inanimate and bearing masculine or feminine appellations, transgressed their natural bounds and were completely possessed by lust).

धरी न काहूँ धीर सब के कन मनसिज हरे।
जे राखे रधुवीर ते उवरे तेहि काल कहुँ।।८५।।

(Nobody could remain self-possessed: the hearts of all were stolen by the god of love. They alone could hold their own against him, to whom the Hero of Raghu's race extended His protection).

सकल कला करि कोरि विधि हारेउ सेन समेत।
चली न अचल समाधि सिव कोपेउ हृदयनिकेत।।८६।।

(The god of love with his army of followers exhausted all his numberless stratagems; Siva's unbroken trance, however, could not be disturbed. This made cupid angry).

अब तें रति तब नाथ कर होइहि नामु अनंगु।
विनु बपु वयापिहि सबहि पुनि सुनु निज मिलन प्रसंगु।।८७।।

(Henceforth, O Rati, your husband shall be called by the name of Ananga (bodiless); he shall dominate all even without a body. Now hear how will meet him again).

सकल सुरन्ह के हृदयँ अस संकर परम उछाहु।
निज नयनन्हि देखा यहहिं नाथ तुम्हार बिनाहु।।८८।।

(The heart of all the immortals is seized with a dominating impulse. They long to witness your wedding with their own eyes, my lord).

कहा हमार न सुनेहु तब नारद के उपदेस।
अब भा झूठ तुम्हार पन जारेउ कामु महेस।।८६।।

(Relying on the advice of Narada you would not heed our remonstrances then. Your bow has failed now; for the great Lord Siva has burnt the god of love !)

हियँ हरेष मुनि बचन सुनि देखि प्रीति विस्वास।
चले भवानिहि नाइ सिर गए हिमालय पास।।६०।।

(Hearing the words of Bhavani and perceiving her devotion and faith, the sages were gladdened at heart. Bowing their head to Her, they went to Himavan).

लगे सवांरन सकल सुर बाहन विविध विमान।
होहि सगुन मंगल सुभद करहिं अपछरा गान।।६१।।

(All the gods began to adorn their vehicles and aerial cars of various kinds, happy and auspicious omens were visible and celestial damsels sang for joy).

विष्नु कहा अस बिहसि तब बोलि सकल दिसिराज।
बिलग बिलग होइ चलहु सब निज निज सहित समाज।।६२।।

(God Visnu then called all the guardians of the different quarters and smilingly said, "Everyone of you should march separately each with his own retinue").

नाचहि गावहि गीत परम तरंगी भूत सब।
देखत अति विपरीत बोलहिं बचन विचित्र विधि।।६३।।

(The ghosts danced and sung, they were all extremely fantastic. They looked most absurd and spoke words in a peculiar style).

जगदवं जहँ अवतरी जसे पुरू वरनि कि जाइ।
रिद्धि सिद्धि संपति सुख नित नूतन अधिकाइ।।६४।।

(The city in which the Mother of the universe had bodied Herself forth baffled all description. Prosperity and success, wealth and happiness were always on the increase there and presented a new aspect).

समुझि महेस समाज सब जननि जनक मुसुकाहि।
बाल बुझाइ विविध विधि निडर होहु डरू नाहिं।।६५।।

(The parents smiled; for they knew that the children were taking of Siva's retinue. They reassured the children in many ways and said, "Be not afraid, there is no cause for fear").

भई बिकल अबला सकल दुखित देखि गिरिनारि।
करि बिलापु रोदति वदति सुता सनेहु संभारि।।६६।।

(All the ladies assembled there were distressed when they saw the consort of Himacala sad. Recalling the affection of her daughter she wailed, wept and exclaimed as below).

तेहि अवसर नारद सहित अरू रिषि सप्त समेत।
समाचार सुनि तुहिनगिरि गवने तुरत निकेत।।६७।।

(On hearing the news that very moment Himacala came to his house along with Narada and the seven seers).

सुनि नारद के बचन तब सब कर मिटा विषाद।
छन महुँ ब्यापउ सकल पुर घर घर यह संवाद।।६८।।

(When they heard Narada's explanation, the sadness of all was dispersed. In a trice the news spread from house to house throughout the city).

बहुरि मुनिन्ह हिमवंत कहुँ लगन सुनाई आइ।
समय विलोकि विवाह कर पठए देव बोलाइ।।९९।।

(The seven sages called once more and read out to Himavan the note recording the time fixed for the wedding; and perceiving that the hour had arrived, the latter sent for the gods).

मुनि अनुसासन गनपतिहि पूजेउ संभु भवानि।
कोउ सुनि संसय करै जनि सुर अनादि जिपँ जानि।।१००।।

(At the direction of the sages Sambhu and Bhavani paid divine honours to Lord Ganapati. Let no one be puzzled to hear this; for one should bear in mind that gods have existed from time without beginning).

नाथ उमा मम प्रान सम गृहकिंकरी करेहु।
छमेहु सकल उपराध अब होइ प्रसन्न वरू देहु।।१०१।।

(Lord Uma is dear to me as life; take her as a maid servant of your house and forgive all her faults. Be pleased to grant this boon to me).

चले संग हिमवंतु तब पहुँचावन अति हेतु।
विविध भाँति परितोषु करि विदा कीन्ह वृषकेतु।।१०२।।

(Himavan then accompanied Siva in order to escort Him with great affection. Siva, however sent him back consoling him in various ways).

चरित सिंधु गिरिजा रमन वेद न पावहिं पारू।
वरनै तुलसीदासु किमि अति मतिमंद गवारूँ।।१०३।।

(The exploits of Girija's lord are illimitable like the ocean; even the Vedas cannot reach their end. How, then, can Tulsidas a most dull-witted clown, succeed in describing them).

प्रथमहि मैं कहि सिव चरित बूझा मरमु तुम्हारा।
सुचि सेवक तुम्ह राम के रहित समस्त विकार।।१०४।।

(Having begun by recounting the deeds of Siva I have come to know your secret. You are indeed a faithful servant of Rama, free from all impurities).

सिद्ध तपोधन जोगिजन सुर किनर मुनिवृंद।
बसहि तहाँ सुकृति सकल सेवहिं सिव सुखकंद।।१०५।।

(Hosts of Siddhas (adepts) ascetics and Yogis (mystics) as well as gods. Kinnaras and sages, all lucky souls, reside there and adore Siva, the root of all joy).

जटा मुकुट सुरसरित सिर लोचन नलिन बिसाल।
नीलकंठ लावन्यनिधि सोइ बालविधु भाल।।१०६।।

(With his twisted coils of hair for a crown and the celestial stream (the Ganga) adoring His head, eyes as big as a pair of lotuses, throat dark with poisson and with the crescent shining on His brow, the Lord looked like a veritable mine of beauty).

प्रभु समरथ सर्वग्य सिव सकल कला गुन धाम।
जोग ग्यान बैराग्य निधि प्रनत कलपतरू नाम।।१०७।।

("My Lord, you are all powerful, all wise, and all blissful, you are a repository of all arts and virtues and a storehouse of yoga (askesis), wisdom and dispassion. Your name is a wish. Yielding tree as it were to the suppliant).

जौं नृप तनय त ब्रह्मा किमि नारि बिरहँ मनि भोरि।
देखि चरित महिमा सुनत भ्रमति बुद्धि अति मोरि।।१०८।।

(If a king's son how could he be Brahma (the infinite)? And if he were Brahma, how could his mind get unhinged by the loss of his wife ? When I see his acts on the one hand, and hear of his glory on the other, my mind gets utterly confused).

बदउँ पद धारि धरनि सिरू विनय करउँ कर जोरि।
बरनहु रघुवर बिसद जसु श्रुति सिद्धांत निचोरि।।१०९।।

(Placing my head on the ground, I adore your feet and entreat you with joined palms to recount the unsullied glory of the chief of Raghus, giving in substance the conclusion of the revealed texts (the Vedas) on the subject)

बहुरि कहहु करूनायतन कीन्ह जो अचरज राम।
प्रजा रहित रधुबंसमनि किमि गवने निज धाम।।११०।।

(Thereafter relate, O gracious Lord, the miracle wrought by Rama viz. how that jewel of Raghu's line proceeded to His divine abode alongwith all his subjects).

मगन ध्यानरस दंड जुग पुनि मन बाहेर कीन्ह।
रघुपति चरित महेस तब हरषित बरनै लीन्ह।।१११।।

(For an honour or so Siva was lost in the ecstasy of meditation. He then recovered Himself and thereafter began joyfully to tell the story of Rama).

राम कृपा तें पारवति सपनेहुँ तब मन माहिं।
सोक मोह संदेह भ्रम मम किचार कछु नाहिं।।११२।।

(By the blessing of Rama, O Parvati, not even in dream can grief, infatuation, doubt or error enter your mind, so far as I can judge).

रामकथा सुरधेनु सम सबत सब सुख दानि।
सतसमाज सुरलोक सब को न सुनै अस जानि।।११३।।

("Like the cow of plenty, the story of Rama bestows all blessings on those who devote themselves to it; and the assemblages of saints are the various abodes of gods. Knowing this, who would not listen to it).

कहहिं सुनहिं अस अद्यम नर ग्रसे जे मोह पिसाच।
पाषंडी हरि पद विमुख जानहिं झूठ न साच।।११४।।

(Such words are spoken and heard by those vile men alone who are possessed by the devil of infatuation, are impious and averse to the feet of Shri Hari and know no difference between truth and falsehood).

अस निज ह्रदयँ बिचारि तजु संसय भजु राम पद।
सुनु गिरिराज कुमारि भ्रम तब रवि कर बचन मम।।११५।।

(Thus assured in your heart, discard all doubt and adore Shri Rama's feet O daughter of the mountain-king, hear my words, which are sun-beams as it were for the darkness of error).

पुरूष प्रसिद्ध प्रकास निधि प्रगट परावर नाथ।
रधुकुलमनि मम स्वामि सोइ कहि सिवँ नायउ माथ।।११६।।

("He who is universally known as the spirit, the fount of light, manifest in all forms and is the lord of life as well as of matter, that jewel of Raghu's line is my Master. So saying Siva boured this head to him).

रजत सीप महुँ भास जिमि जथा भानु कर बारि।
जदपि मृषा तिहुँ काल सोइ भ्रम न सकइ कोउ रारि।।११७।।

(Just as a shell is mistaken for silver and a mirage for water even though the appearance is false at all times (in the past, present and future), nobody can dispel this delusion).

जेहि इमि गावहिं बेद बुध जाहि धरहिं मुनि ध्यान।
सोइ दसरथ सुत भगत हित कोसलपति भगवान।।११८।।

(He who is thus extolled by the Vedas and men of wisdom and whom the sages love to contemplate is no other than the divine Rama, son of Dasrath, lord of Ayodhya, the friend of His devotees).

पुनि पुनि प्रभु पद कमल गहि जोरि पंकरूह पानि।
बोलीं गिरिजा बचन बर मनहुँ प्रेम रस सानि।।११९।।

(Clasping the lotus feet of her lord again and again, and joining her lotus like palms, Parvati spoke the following fine words, steeping them as it were in the nectar of love).

हियँ हरषे कामारि तब संकर सहज सुजान।
बहु विधि उमहि प्रसंसि पुनि बोले कृपानिधान।।१२०क।।

(The all merciful and all wise Sankara, the Destroyer of Cupid, was glad at heart and, extolling Uma in so many ways, said):

सुन सुभ कथा भवानि रामचरितमानस विमल।
कहा भुसुंडि बटवानि सुना बिहग नायक गरूड़।।१२०ख।।

सो संवाद उदार जेहि विधि भा आगे कहव।
सुनहु राम अवतार चरित परम सुन्दर अनध।।१२०ग।।

हरि गुन नाम अपार कथा रूप अगनित अमित।
मैं निज मति अनुसार कहउँ उमा सादर सुनहु।।१२०घ।।

(Hear the blessed story of the holy Ramacharitmanas, which was narrated at length by the sage Bhusandi and heard by the king of birds, Garuda. I shall tell you later on how that great dialogue took place. First listen to the most charming and sanctifying story of His descent. The virtues, names, stories and forms of Shri Hari are all unlimited, innumerable and immeasurable. Yet I proceed to tell them according to the best of my intellectual capacity; listen Uma with reverence).

असुर मारि थापहिं सुरन्ह राखहिं निज श्रुति सेतु।
जग बिस्तारहिं बिसद जस राम जन्म कर हेतु।।१२१।।

(Killings the demons He reinstates the gods, preserves the bounds of propriety fixed by the Vedas, which represent His own breath, and diffuses His immaculate glory throughout the world. This is the motive of Shri Rama's descent).

भए निसाचर जाइ तेइ महावीर बलवान।
कुंभकरण रावन सुभट सुर बिजई जग जान।।१२२।।

(It is these two brothers that were born again as powerful and most valiant Raksasas. Ravana and Kumbhakarna, who were great warriors and as all the world knows, conquered even gods).

छल करि टारेउ तासु ब्रत प्रभु सुर कारज कीन्ह।
जब तेहि जानेउ मरम तब श्राप कोप करि दीन्ह।।१२३।।

(By a stratagem the Lord broke her vow of chastity and accomplished the purpose of the gods. When the lady discovered the trick, she cursed Him in her wrath).

बोले बिहसि महेस तब ग्यानी मूढ़ न कोइ।
जेहि जस रघुपति करहिं जब सो तस तेहि छन होइ।।१२४क।।

(The great Lord Siva then replied with a smile. There is no one enlightened or deluded. Man instantly becomes what the Lord of Raghus wills him to be at a particular moment).

कहउँ राम गुन गाथ भरद्वाज सादर सुनहु।
भव भंजन रघुनाथ भजु तुलसी तजि मान मद।।१२४ख।।

(Said Yajnavalkya, "I am going to recount the virtues of Rama, O Bharadvaja; listen with a devout mind". Renouncing pride and intoxication. O Tulsidas adore the Lord of Raghus, who puts an end to metempsychosis).

सूख हाड़ लै भाग सठ स्वान निरखि मृगराज।
छीनि लेइ जनि जान जड़ तिमि सुरपतिहि न लाज।।१२५।।

(Just as a foolish dog, on seeing a king of beasts, should run away with a dry bone, fearing in his crass ignorance lest the lion should rob him of it, Indira too in his shamelessness thought as above).

सहित सहाय सभीत अति मानि हारि मन मैन।
गहेसि जाइ मुनि चरन तब कहि सुठि आरत बैन।।१२६।।

(In the dismay the god of love with his accomplices acknowledged his defeat and clasped the sages feet, addressing him in accents of deep humility).

संभु दीन्ह उपदेस हित नहिं नारदहि सोहान।
भरद्वाज कौतुक सुनहु हरि इच्छा बलवान।।१२७।।

(Wholesome was the advice given by Sambhu, but it did not please Narada. Bharadvaja, now hear what interesting thing happened. The will of Hari is predominant).

रूख बदन करि बचन मृदु बोले श्रीभगवान।
तुम्हरे सुमिरन तें मिटहिं मोह मार मद मान।।१२८।।

(With an impassive look, yet in coaxing accent, said the Lord, "By your very thought self delusion, lust, arrogance and pride disappear").

बिरचेउ मग महुँ नगर तेहिं सत जोजन बिस्तार।
श्रीनिवासपुर ते अधिक रचना विविध प्रकार।।१२६।।

(The Lords Maya (deluding potency) created on the way a city with an area of eight hundred square miles. The manifold architectural beauties of that city excelled even those of Visnu's own capital (Vaikuntha).

आनि देखाई नारदहि भूपति राजकुमारि।
कहहु नाथ गुन दोष सब एहि के हृदयँ विचारि।।१३०।।

(The king brought and showed the princess to Narada and said, "Tell me after mature thought all that is good or bad about her").

एहि अवसर चाहिअ परम सोभा रूप विसाल।
जो विलोकि रीझै कुआँरि तब मेलै जयमाल।।१३१।।

("What is needed on this occasion is great personal charm and surpassing beauty. Whereby the Princess may be enamoured of me and place the wreath of victory round my neck", he continued).

जेहि विधि होइहि परम हित नारद सुनहु तुम्हार।
सोइ हम करब न आन कछु बचन न मृषा हमार।।१३२।।

("Narada listen to me, I shall do that alone which is good to you, and nothing else. My words can never be untrue").

रहे तहाँ दुइ रूद्र गान ते जानहिं सब भेउ।
बिप्रबेष देखत फिरहिं परम कौतुकी तेउ।।१३३।।

(Two of Siva's attendants too happened to be there. They knew the whole secret and disguised as Brahmanas, went about seeing the fun).

सखी संग लैं कुवाँरि तब चलि जनु राजमराल।
देखत फिरइ महीप सब कर सरोज जयमाल।।१३४।।

(Accompanied by her girl companions the princess then glided as a swan. With a wreath of victory in her lotus hands she moved about surveying each of her royal suitors).

होहु निसाचर जाइ तुम्ह कपटी पापी दोउ।
हंसेहु हमहि सो लेहु फल बहुरि हँसेहु मुनि कोउ।।१३५।।

("O you sinful imposters, go and be reborn as demons. You mocked me; therefore, reap its reward. Mock again a sage, if you do").

असुर सुरा बिष संकरहि आपु रमा मनि चारू।
स्वारथ साधक कुटिल तुम्ह सदा कपट व्यवहारू।।१३६।।

(Apportioning intoxicating liquor to the demons and poison to Sankara. You appropriated Rama and the lovely gem (Kaustublia) to yourself. You have never been selfish and perverse, and treacherous in your dealings).

श्राप सीस धरि हरषि हियँ प्रभु बहु विनती कीन्हि।
निज माया कै प्रबलता करषि कृपनिधि लीन्हि।।१३७।।

(Gladly accepting the curse, the compassionate Lord made many entreaties to the sage, and withdrew the irresistible charm of His Maya).

बहुविधि मुनिहि प्रबोधि प्रभु तब भए अंतरधान।
सत्यलोक नारद चले करत राम गुन गान।।१३८।।

(Having thus reassured the sage, the Lord then disappeared, while Narad proceeded to Satyaloka (the seventh paradise, the abode of Brahma) chanting Shri Rama's praises as he went).

एक कलप एहि हेतु प्रभु लीन्ह मनुज अवतार।
सुर रंजन सज्जन सुखद हरि भंजन भुवि भार।।१३९।।

(In one Kalpa (round of creation) it was for this reason that Lord Sri Hari assumed a human form. It is His vow to gladden the gods, to delight the virtuous and to ease the earth of its burden).

सुर नर मुनि कोउ नाहिं जेहि न मोह माया प्रबल।
अस बिचारि मन माहिं भजिअ महामाया पतिहि।।१४०।।

(There is no god, man or sage whom Shri Hari's powerful Maya cannot infatuate. Bearing this in mind, one should adore the Lord of this great Maya).

सो मैं तुम्ह सन कहउँ सबु सुनु मुनीस मन लाइ।
राम कथा कलि मल हरनि मंगल करनि सुहाइ।।१४१।।

(I proceeded to tell you all about it, O Bharadvaja; listen attentively. The story of Shri Rama wipes out all the impurities of the Kali age, brings forth all blessings and is most charming).

होइ न विषय बिराग भवन बसत भा चौथपन।
हृदयँ बहुत दुख लाग जनम गयउ हरिभगति बिनु।।१४२।।

("I have reached the fourth stage of my life (old age) while I am still living under the roof of my house as a householder, but I have not yet lost my relish for the pleasures of sense", he said to himself. He felt sore distressed at heart that his life had been wasted without devotion to Shri Hari).

द्वादस अच्छर मंत्र पुनि जपहिं सहित अनुराग।
बासुदेव पद पंकरूह दंपति मन अति लाग।।१४३।।

(The further devoutely repeated the twelve lettered formula (ॐ नमो भगवते वासुदेवाय) Their mind was foundly devoted to the lotus feet of Lord Vasudeva (the all pervading Vishnu)).

एहि विधि बीते बरष षट सहस वारि आहार।
संवत सप्त सहस्र पुनि रहे समीर आधार।।१४४।।

(In this way six thousand years elapsed even while they lived on water. Then for another seven millennia they lived on air alone).

श्रवन सुधा सम वचन सुनि पुलक प्रफुल्लित गात।
बोले मनु करि दंडवत प्रेम न हृदयँ समात।।१४५।।

(As the royal couple heard these words, which were delightful to the ear as nectar itself, the hair on their body bristled and a thrill ran through their limbs. Then, falling prostrate on the ground and with his heart overflowing with love Manu spoke).

नील सरोरूह नील मनि नील नीरधर स्याम।
लाजहिं नत सोभा निरखि कोटि कोटि सत काम।।१४६।।

(Billions and millions of Loves blushed to behold the elegance of His swarthy form, which resembled a blue lotus (in the softness of its touch), a sapphire (in its gloss) and a dark cloud (in its freshness).

तड़ित बिनिंदक पीत पर उरद रेख बर तीनि।
नाभि मनोहर लेति जनु जमुन भँवर छवि छीनि।।१४७।।

(His yellow robes put to shame streaks of lightning and His belly had three folds; while His attractive naved robbed,as it were, the eddies on the Yamuna of their beauty).

बोले कृपानिधान पुनि अति प्रसन्न मोहि जानि।
मागहु वर जोइ भाव मन महादानि अनुमानि।।१४८।।

(The compassionate Lord then said, "knowing that I am highly pleased with you and recognizing Me as a great donor, ask whatever boon you will").

दानि सिरोमनि कृपानिधि नाथ कहउँ सतिमाउ।
चाहउँ तुम्हहि समान सुत प्रभु सन कवन दुराउ।।१४९।।

("O crest-jewel of donors O gracious Lord, I tell you my sincere wish: I would have a son like you. I can have nothing to conceal from you").

सोइ सुख सोइ गति सोइ भगति सोइ निज चरन सनेहु।
सोइ विवेक सोइ रहनि प्रभु हमहि कृपा करि देहु।।१५०।।

("Gant me in your mercy, O Lord, that very bliss, the same destiny,the same devotion, the same attachment to your feet, the same insight and the same mode of living").

तहँ करि भोग विसाल तात गएँ कछु काल पुनि।
होइहहु अवध भुआल तब मैं होव तुम्हार सुत।।१५१।।

(Having enjoyed extensive enjoyments there you shall, after some time, be born as king of Ayodhya: then, dear father, I will be your son).

यह इतिहास पुनीत अति उमहि कही वृषकेतु।
भरद्वाज सुनु अपर पुनि राम जनम कर हेतु।।१५२।।

(This most sacred legend was related by Siva (who has a bull emblazoned on His standard) to Uma. Bharadvaja now hear yet another cause of Shri Rama's birth).

जब प्रतापरवि भमउ नृप फिरी दोहाई देस।
प्रजा पाल अति वेदविधि कतहुँ नहीं अघ लेस।।१५३।।

(When Pratapabhanu became king, a proclamation to this effect was made throughout the land. He looked after his subjects with utmost care according to the precepts of the Vedas and there was not a speck of sin anywhere (in his kingdom).

स्ववस बिस्व करि बाहुबल निज पुर कीन्ह प्रवेसु।
अरथ धरम कामादि सुख सेवइ समयँ नरेसु।।१५४।।

(Having thus subjugated the whole universe by the might of his arm, the king re-entered his capital. He devoted himself to the pleasures of wealth, religious practices and sense gratification etc. at the appropriate time).

जहँ लगि कहे पुरान श्रुति एक एक सब जाग।
बार सहस्र सहस्र नृप किए सहित अनुराग।।१५५।।

(Whatever sacrifices have been enjoined in the Vedas and the Puranas, the king devoutly performed each one of them a thousand times).

नील महीधर सिखर सम देखि बिसाल बराहु।
चपरि चलेउ हय सुटुकि नृप हाँकि न होइ निवाहु।।१५६।।

(On seeing the huge boar, which resembled a purple mountain-peak the king whipped the horse and advanced rapidly, challenging the boar at the same time and saying it could no longer escape).

खेद खिन्न छुद्धित तृषित राजा वाजि समेत।
खोजत व्याकुल सरित सर जल बिनु भयउ अचेत।।१५७।।

(Exhausted with much exertion and oppressed by hunger and thirst, the king and his horse kept searching for a stream or pond and almost fainted for want of water).

भूपति तृषित बिलोकि तेहि सरबरू दीन्ह देखाइ।
मज्जन पान समेत हय कीन्ह नृपति हरषाइ।।१५८।।

(Seeing King Pratapbhanu thirsty, he showed him a good lake and the king as well as his horse gladly bathed in it and drank from it).

निसा धोर गम्भीर बन पंथ न सुनहु सुजान।
बसहु आजु अस जानि तुम्ह जाएहुँ होत विहान।।१५९।।

("Listen, O friend: dark and dreary is the night, and the forest is dense and trackless; knowing this, tarry here overnight and depart next morning").

तुलसी जसि भवतव्यता तैसी मिलइ सहाइ।
आपुनु आवइ ताहि पहिं ताहि तहाँ लै जाइ।।१५६ख।।

(The inevitable, says Tulsidas, is invariably preceded by circumstances that are favourable to it. Either it comes to a man or takes him to the cause of his doom).

कपट बोरि बानी मृदुल बोलेउ जुगुति समेत।
नाम हमार भिखारि अब निर्धन रहित निकेत।।१६०।।

(He uttered the following soft yet false and artful words. My name is now Bhikhari (a mendicant), penniless and homeless as I am).

अब लगि मोहि न मिलेउ कोउ मैं न जनावउँ काहु।
लोकमान्यता अनल सम कर तप कानन दाहु।।१६१क।।

(No one has come to me so far nor do I make myself known to anyone, for popular esteem is like a wild fire, which consumes the forest of penance i.e. neutralizes it).

तुलसी देखि सुबषु भूलहिं मूढ़ न चतुर नर।
सुंदर केकिहि पेखु वचन सुधा राम असन अहि।।१६१ख।।

("Not only fools", says Tulsidas, "but even clever men are taken in by fair appearances: Look at the beautiful peacock; though its notes are sweet like nectar, it devours snakes).

आदिसृष्टि उपजी जबहिं तब उतपति भै मोरि।
नाम एकतनु हेतु तेहि देह न धरी बहोरि।।१६२।।

("My birth took place at the first dawn of creation. Since then I have never taken another body; that is why I am called Ekatanu").

सुनु महीस असि नीति जहँ तहँ नाम न कहहिं नृप।
मोहि तोहि पर अति प्रीति सोइ चतुरता विचारि तब।।१६३।।

("O King, the political maxim is that kings should not disclose their name in all cases. And when I thought of your political sagacity, I conceived great love for you").

जरा मरन दुख रहित तनु समर जितै जानि कोउ।
एकछत्र रिपुहीन महि राज कलप सत होउ।।१६४।।

("Let my body be free from old age, death and suffering; let no one vanquish me in battle and let me enjoy undisputed sovereignty over the globe for a hundred Kalpas (repetitions of creation) and let me have no enemies).

एवमस्तु कहि कपटमुनि बोला कुटिल बहोरि।
मिलब हमार भुलाव निज कहहु त हमहि न खोरि।।१६५।।

("Amen !" said the false anchorite, and added with crafty intent, "if you tell anyone about my meeting with you and your straying away, the fault shall not be mine").

होहिं बिप्र बस कवन विधि कहहु कृपा करि सोउ।
तुम्ह तजि दीनदयाल निज हितु न देखउँ कोउ।।१६६।।

(How shall I be able to win over the Brahmans ? Kindly tell me that too. I see no friend other than you, my gracious lord).

अस कहि गहे नरेस पद स्वामी होहु कृपाल।
मोहि लागि दुख सहिअ प्रभु सज्जन दीनदयाल।।१६७।।

(So saying, the king clasped the hermits feet and said, "Be gracious to me, my master. You are a saint, compassionate to the humble; therefore, my lord, take this trouble on my behalf).

नित नूतन द्विज सहस सत बरेहु सहित परिवार।
मैं तुम्हारे संकलप लगि दिनहिं करवि जवनार।।१६८।।

("Everyday invite a new set of a hundred thousand Brahmanas with their families; while I, so long as your vow lasts, shall provide the daily banquet").

मैं आउव सोइ बेषु धरि पहिचानेहु तब मोहि।
जब एकांत बोलाइ सब कथा सुनावौं तोहि।।१६६।।

("I will come in the form I have told you, and you will recognize me when I call you aside and remind you of all this")?

रिपु तेजसी अकेल अपि लधु करि गनिअ न ताहु।
अजहुँ देत दुख रवि ससिहि सिर अवसेषित राहु।।१७०।।

(A spirited foe, even though left alone, should not be lightly regarded. The demon Rahu, who has nothing left of him but his head, is able to torment both the sun and moon even to this day).

राजा के उपरोहितहि हरि लै गयउ बहोरि।
लै राखेसि गिरि खोह महुँ मायाँ करि मति मोरि।।१७१।।

(Again he carried off the kings family priest and, depriving him of his senses by his supernatural power, kept him in a mountain cave).

नृप हरषउ पहिचानि गुरू भ्रम बस रहा न चेत।
बरे तुरत सत सहस बर विप्र कुटुबं समेत।।१७२।।

(The king was delighted to recognize his preceptor (in the priests' form); his mind was too clouded to have any sense left. At once he invited a hundred thousand chosen Brahmanas with their families).

बोले विप्र सकोप तब नहिं कछु कीन्ह बिचार।
जाइ निसाचर होहु नृप मूढ़ सहित परिवार।।१७३।।

(Then exclaimed the Brahmanas in wrath, regardless of consequences "O foolish king go and take birth in the demon's form, you and all your family").

भूपति भावी मिटइ नहिं जदपि न दूषन तोर।
किएँ अन्यथा होइ नहिं बिप्रश्राप अति धोर।।१७४।।

("Even though you are guiltless, O king, what is inevitable fails not. A Brahmana's curse is very terrible, no amount of effort can counteract it").

भरद्वाज सुनु जाहि जब होइ विधाता नाम।
धूरि मेरूसम जनक जम ताहि ब्यालसम दाम।।१७५।।

(Listen O Bhardvaja; whosoever incurs the displeasure of heaven, for him a grain of dust becomes vast as Mount Meru, a father becomes frightful as Yama (the god of death) and every rope a snake).

उपजे जदपि पुलसत्यकुल पावन अमल अनूप।
तदपि महीसुर श्राप बस भए सकल अधरूप।।१७६।।

(Even though they were born in the incomparably pure and holy line of the sage Pulsatya, yet on account of the Brahmana's curse, they were all embodiments of sin).

गए विभीषन पास पुनि कहेउ पुत्र बर मागु।
तेहिं मागेउ भगवंत पद कमल अमल अनुरागु।।१७७।।

(Last of all Brahma went up to Vibhisana and said, "Ask a boon my son". He asked for pure love for the lotus feet of the Lord).

खाई सिंधु गंभीर अति चारिहुँ दिसि फिरि आव।
कनक कोट मनिखचित दृढ़ बरनि न जाइ बनाव।।१७८क।।

हरि प्रेरित जेहिं कलप जोइ जातु धानपति होइ।
सूर प्रतापी अतुलबल दल समेत बस सोइ।।१७८ख।।

(The ocean surrounded it on all sides as a very deep moat. It had a strong fortification well built of gold and jewels, the architectural beauty of which defied description. Whoever was preordained by Shri Hari to the chief of the demons in a particular cycle, that illustrious hero of incomparable might lived there with his army).

कौतुकहीं कैलास पुनि लीव्हेसि जाइ उठाइ।
मनहुँ तौलि निज बाहुबल चला बहुत सुख पाइ।।१७६।।

(Again in a sportive mood he went and lifted Mount Kailas and, thereby testing as it were the might of his arms, returned most jubilant).

कुमुख अकंपन कुलिसरद धुमकेतु अतिकाय।
एक एक जग जीति सक ऐसे सुभट निकाय।।१८०।।

(There were many more champions such as the hideous Kumukha, the interpid Akampana, Kulisarada with teeth like thunderbolts the fiery Dhumketu and the gigantic Atikaya, each one of whom was able to subdue the whole world).

छुधा छीन बलहीन सुर सहजेहिं मिलिहहिं आइ।
तब मारिहउँ कि छाड़िहउँ भली भान्ति अपनाइ।।१८१।।

(Emaciated with starvation and rendered weak, the gods will automatically surrender to me. Then I will see whether I should kill them or let them go after subjecting them perfectly to my will).

भुजबल बिस्व बस्य करि राखेसि कोउ न सुतंत्र।
मंडलीक मनि रावन राज करइ निज मंत्र।।१८२क।।

देव जच्छ गंधर्व नर किनर नाग कुमारि।
जीति बदीं निज बाहुबल बहु सुन्दर बर नारि।।१८२ख।।

(By his mighty arm he subdued the whole universe and left no one independent. The king of kings, Ravana, ruled according to his own will. He won by the might of his arms and weded daughters of gods, yaksas, Gandharvas, human beings, Kinnars and Nagas and many other beautiful and excellent dames).

बरनि न जाइ अनीति धोर निसाचर जो करहिं।
हिंसा पर अति प्रीति तिन्ह के पापहि कवनि मिति।।१८३।।

(The terrible outrages the demons did beggar description. There is no limit to the evil-doings of those who hold violence most dear to their heart).

धरनि धरहिं मन धीर कह विरंचि हरिपद सुमिरू।
जानत जन की पीर प्रभु भंजिहि दारून विपति।।१८४।।

("Have patience, Earth", said Brahma, "and fix your mind on the feet of Shri Hari. The Lord knows the distress of His servants and will put an end to your terrible suffering").

सुनि विरंचि मन हरष तन पुलकि नयन बह नीर।
अस्तुति करत जोरि कर सावधान मति धीर।।१८५।।

(Brahma was glad at heart to hear. My words the hair on his body bristled and tears flowed from his eyes. Recovering himself, the stable minded Brahma joined his palms and prayed).

जानि सभय सुरभूमि सुनि बचन समेत सनेह।
गगनगिरा गंभीर भइ हरनि सोक संदेह।।१८६।।

(Knowing that the gods and Earth were terror sticken and hearing their loving entreaties, a deep voice came from heaven, which removed all their doubt and anxiety).

निज लोकहिं विंरचि गे देवन्ह इहइ सिखाइ।
वानर तनु धरि धरि महि हरि पद सेवहु जाइ।।१८७।।

(Then Brahma proceeded to his realm after thus instructing the gods; "Assuming the form of monkeys you go to the earth and adore the feet of Shri Hari").

कौसल्यादि नारि प्रिय सब आचरन पुनीत।
पति अनुकूल प्रेम दृढ़ हरि पद कमल विनीत।।१८८।।

(Kausalya and his other beloved consorts were all of holy life, humble and devoted to their lord, they had a strong attachment to the lotus feet of Shri Hari).

तब अदृस्य भए पावक सकल समहि समुझाइ।
परमानंद मगन नृप हरष न ह्रदयँ समाइ।।१८६।।

(The fire god then disappeared after telling the whole assembly of what was to be done. The king was transported with ecstasy and could not contain himself for joy).

जोग लगन ग्रह बार तिथि सकल भए अनुकूल।
चर अरू अचर हर्षजुत राम जन्म सुखमूल।।१९०।।

(The position of the sun and the moon, the zodiacal sign into which the sun had entered, the position of the seven other planets, the day of the week as well as the day of the lunar month, all these turned out to be propitious. And full of delight was all creation, animate and inanimate; for the birth of Shri Rama is the source of joy).

सुर समूह विनती करि पहुँचे निज निज धाम।
जगनिवास प्रभु प्रगटे अखिल लोक विश्राम।।१९१।।

(Having offered their praises the gods returned to their several abodes, when the Lord, the abode of the universe and the solace of all creation, manifested Himself).

बिप्र धेनु सुर संत हित लीन्ह मनुज अवतार।
निज इच्छा निर्मित तनु माया गुन गो पार।।१९२।।

(For the sake of Brahmanas, cows, gods and saints, the Lord, who transcends Maya and is beyond the three modes of Prakrti (Sattva, Rajas and Tamasa) as well as beyond the reach of the senses took birth as a man assuming a form which is a product of His own will).

नंदीमुख सराध करि जातकरम सब कीन्ह।
हाटक धेनु बसन मनि नृप बिप्रन्ह कहँ दीन्ह।।१९३।।

(After performing the Nandimukha Sraddha the king completed all the rites connected with the birth of a child and made gifts of gold, cows, raiment and jewels to the Brahmanas).

गृह गृह बाज बधाव सुभ प्रगटे सुषमा कंद।
हरषवंत सब जहँ तहँ नगर नारि नर ब्रृंद।।१९४।।

(There was happy music of festivity in every house; for the very fountain of beauty had manifested Himself. All the men and women of the city were full of joy everywhere).

मास दिवस कर दिवस भा मरम न जानइ कोइ।
रथ समेत रवि थाकेउ निसा कवन विधि होइ।।१९५।।

(The day assumed the length of a month, but no one could understand the mystery. The sun stood motionless with his chariot; how could there be any night).

मन संतोषे सबन्हि के जहँ तहँ देहिं असीस।
सकल तनय चिर जीवहुँ तुलसीदास के ईस।।१९६।।

(All were satisfied in their heart and invoked blessings here and there, saying, "May all the sons of Dasaratha live long those Lord of Tulsidas").

लच्छन धाम राम प्रिय सकल जगत आधार।
गुरू बसिष्ट तेहि राखा लछिमन नाम उदार।।१९७।।

(He who is the abode of noble characteristics, the beloved of Shri Rama and the mainstay of the whole universe, was given by Guru Vasistha the splendid name of Lakshmana).

व्यापक ब्रह्मा निरंजन निर्गुन बिगत विनोद।
सो अज प्रेम भगति बस कौसल्या के गोद।।१९८।।

(The unborn and all prevailing Brahma, who is untainted by Maya, without attributes and devoid of play, has sought shelter in the arms of Kausalaya conquered by her love and devotion).

सुख संदोह मोहपर ग्यान गिरा गोतीत।
दंपति परम प्रेम बस कर सिसुचरित पुनीत।।१९९।।

(The all-blissful Lord, who is above delusion and transcends knowledge, speech and all sensuous perception, sported like an innocent child, yielding to the supreme love of the royal couple (Dasaratha and Kausalaya).

प्रेम मगन कौसल्या निसि दिन जात न जान।
सुत सनेह बस माता बालचरित कर गान।।२००।।

(Kausalaya remained so rapt in love that days and nights passed unnoticed. Out of affection for her boy she would sing lays of His childhood).

INDEX

D

E

F

G

H

I

J

□□□